The Bottom Line

BRUCE ANDREW JONES

The Bottom Line.
Copyright © 2017, 2021 by Bruce Andrew Jones.

All rights reserved. No part of this book may be reproduced in any form or by any electronic or mechanical means, including information storage and retrieval systems, without permission in writing from the publisher and author, except by reviewers, who may quote brief passages in a review.

This publication contains the opinions and ideas of its author. It is intended to provide helpful and informative material on the subjects addressed in the publication. The author and publisher specifically disclaim all responsibility for any liability, loss, or risk, personal or otherwise, which is incurred as a consequence, directly or indirectly, of the use and application of any of the contents of this book.

First originally published by Page Publishing, Inc. 2017

ISBN: 978-1-63950-098-7   [Paperback Edition]
      978-1-63950-099-4   [eBook Edition]

Printed and bound in The United States of America.

Gateway Towards Success

8063 MADISON AVE #1252
Indianapolis, IN 46227
+13176596889

www.writersapex.com

Contents

Acknowledgments 7

Childhood 11, 43
    Drugs and Alcohol 17
    Drug Experience 1 18
    Drug Experience 2 18
    Drugs Experience 3 20
Rehabilitation 23
Women 24
Job 25
Sex 26
Job (Words of Wisdom) 27
Rules to Abide by to Succeed 28
Staten Island (the Rock) New Brighton:
Domestic Violence (Beating Women) 34
Women 34, 36, 38
Streets 36
Dating 37
Religion 38
Watch for the Setup 39
One of My Favorite Girlfriends: Loved One vs. Cancer 41
Another Favorite Girlfriend 42
Cars 44
Court Date (DWI) 47
Incarceration in DC Jail (May 17, 2010 to June 14, 2010) 53
Traffic Court 60

Helping Hands and Shoot-Out 61
Getting Cigarettes for Girlfriend 62
Child Support: Baby Momma Drama (Do the Right Thing) 63
Words of Wisdom 63, 71
Personal Conduct: Rules for Success 70
Managing Money (Spending Money While Saving Money) 72
Money and Charity-Giving 72
Managing Money (Credit) 73
Domestic Violence 78

About the Author 82

This book is dedicated to all my family, especially my mother, Lillian C. Jones (Ma Dukes); sister Lisa; baby sister Denise (Dee-Dee); Moses Andrew Jones (Jack), my father who is now deceased (God bless him). I thank him for his straightforward and truthful ways. I would not be where I am without him. Thank you, Daddy. RIP. Love you.

Stepfather Elijah Croom, God bless you, and thanks for all the wonderful times and words of wisdom, especially during my brief thirty-day stay of confinement. Thanks for being there. I miss you, and the weekend gatherings haven't been the same since. RIP, Pop. Love you.

Also, special thanks to my long-time close friends of thirty years or more. It's been a heck of a ride. God bless you and your families.

Acknowledgments

God bless all former employees and my coworkers at FBI Headquarters, which is my first government job. Also, God bless all employees and my coworkers at the United States Postal Service in Washington, DC, and worldwide. Keep delivering with urgency the US mail, postal family.

God Bless the following and their families:
Retired Sergeant Derek D Hamilton aka HAMP
Retired Detective Cornell Huddleston aka CHILI
Coworker Carl Briscoe aka BRIS
Coworker Everett Kendall aka E
Coworker and basketball buddy, Ronald Perry aka P

Best Female Friend Saundra Tabron (Little Baby), thanks. God bless you. Also, Page Publishing, thank you for everything. Brenda Carswell, thanks for being there during my last six months of high school by giving me somewhere to live so I could finish and graduate on time. God bless you.

Far East Motors Silver Spring Maryland, a great car service repair center, thank you. Jon, Paul, Watchman, mechanic Eddie, and the rest of the shop, thanks for servicing my Lexus. Keep up the good work.

Also, thanks to the Prince Georges County Md. Library system Hyattsville Branch main Library.

A very special thanks to coworker and ex-girlfriend Lisa Brown-Mcneil English major and university of Maryland Graduate thanks a million literally.

To my favorite aunt, Dorothy Price, thanks for all the good family hospitality throughout the years when I came home to visit often when I was younger. God Bless you. Love you, AKA (DOT).

Solomon Goodwin, my coworker, best friend, hanging partner, RIP. It hasn't been the same since the Lord called you home. God bless you, soul man. Highly decorated 2 branch military veteran and Gulf war vet.

Fifteen years ago, we experienced the Anthrax attack in our then named Brentwood Mail Facility. We lost two of our beloved friends and co-workers, Joseph Curseen, Jr. and Thomas Morris, Jr. Our postal facility was rightfully renamed the Curseen-Morris Processing and Distribution Center (P&DC). The loss of our brothers has forever changed the safety procedures and protocol that now comes into place in making our postal facility and facilities around the country a safer place to work. We will never forget. God Bless these heroes and their families.

I want to give a shout out and praise to my co-workers and fellow craft employees throughout the United States Postal Service especially in the Washington, DC Area Local 305. The Few, The Proud, The Mail Handlers at Curseen-Morris Processing and Distribution Center (P&DC). Keep moving the mail. Doing what we do.

Congratulations to my son and his wife Jaron and Melissa Jones on the birth of my first grandsons' twin boys Lorenzo and Anthony. God Bless them.

God Bless my god daughter Deira Peoples. God daddy loves you.

Stepfather KC Johnson thanks for the street knowledge when I was what you used call a New York Jitterbug and especially for the survival prison lessons which later came in handy thanks again Love you.

Favorite cousin Gerald K Williams aka Gee Money. Love u first and favorite Cuz!

A very special thanks to my Great kind helpful good friend and the best friend an the best neighbor any one can have W.W. thanks for everything NYC. God bless you and your family.

Face it! Nobody owes you a living. What you achieve or fail to achieve in your lifetime is directly related to what you do or fail to do.

No one chooses his parents or childhood, but you can choose your own direction. Everyone has problems and obstacles to overcome, but that too is relative to each individual. *Nothing is carved in stone!* You can change anything in your life if you want to badly enough.

Excuses are for losers. Those who take responsibility for their actions are the real winners in life. Winners meet life's challenges head-on, knowing there are no guarantees, and give it all they've got. And they never think it's too late or too early to begin. Time plays no favorites and will pass whether you act or not.

Take control of your life. Dare to dream and take risks. Compete. If you aren't willing to work for your goals, don't expect others to. Believe in yourself.

Childhood

On August 8, 1961, I, Bruce Andrew Jones, was born in Harlem Hospital in New York City. I was born to Moses A. Jones and Lillian C. McAlpine. My father was a truck driver, and my mother a nurse's aide. From what I could remember, I had two hernias and an operation to remove them. Growing up in New York City was a challenge because every day was a struggle to get around peer pressure. It was always competition among friends, family, and anybody else, depending upon the situation. So even as a little kid, your back was against the wall, and there was no breathing room. My siblings consist of two younger sisters, Lisa and Denise. Of course, I had to look after them since I was the oldest and only boy. As far as elementary school, I went to PS 31 in New Brighton on Staten Island, New York. Elementary School was all right, except they always picked on me since I was the blackest kid in school. Of course, I did not like it, but I did not know any better, so it caused many fights with schoolmates.

My nickname was JBBJ (Jet Black Bruce Jones), so you know I was fighting all the time. As I got older, I realized that my teeth had a double row and different from my sisters' teeth. Theirs were straight, so I asked my mom why. She stated that during pregnancy with me, she took pills she was not supposed to, so now I have two problems—being the blackest and having crooked teeth. Boy was that a bummer. And it did not seem that my mother was trying to help any. Therefore, I started to take matters into my own hands by going to the orthodontist, having surgery after surgery. I only had my two sisters at my side, walking and guiding me home after each surgery, since my mother worked for the postal service and could never take off or did not think it was important. The one thing that I knew at a young age is that a decent smile can take you a long way even if you do not have any money. In addition, I like those pretty girls, and I knew I would have to get things in order to be able to attract these pretty girls. When I was in kindergarten, I was putting my hand up girl's dresses. I saw that they liked that even at a young age.

In addition, I was the only little boy in school that had a baldhead haircut every week, so that was another thing to be called names about. Everybody else had Afro haircuts or braids. I was the only one with a baldhead, so now I was the blackest with a baldhead with crooked teeth. It was an uphill battle, especially in New York City, where at that time (and probably still is), style is first and who has the newest gear. For instance, in New York you have to wear Converse, Adidas, or PRO-Keds. The saying goes like this: "If your sneakers slip and slide, get the one with the star on the side, Converse." Any other sneakers than the ones I mentioned were "skips." So now, on top of all of that to deal with, I am wearing the worst sneakers in the neighborhood. Since they are like that now, everyone is kicking dirt on my new skips. All these situations caused a fight. Of course, my father was a weekend alcoholic: sober all week until Friday night. Between Friday and Sunday, my father would be tore down from the floor down, which would cause my father to hit my mother. In addition, you know I did not like that. Therefore, as I got bigger and older, I started to indulge in sports. In junior high school, I played basketball and boxing. My basketball game was at first horrible, but with a lot of practice and seclusion, I became better. The ballplayers in my hood were so good. I at first couldn't play with them at all in the hood, so I went to my high school basketball court to practice alone and sharpen my skills so I could compete in my own neighborhood and be out with my ball-playing friends (which by the way would soon become some of the best ball players in New York City unbeknownst to me). Therefore, once I got my game tight, I came back down to my hood park, which is Mahoney Playground in New

Brighton, Staten Island, New York. I tried out for the summer league in New York, which is citywide. The divisions are as follows: bitties (10–12 years old), midgets (12–14 years old), juniors (15–18 years old), seniors (18 up), unlimited (any age).

I made it to the team but did not get a lot of playing time, so I practiced all winter in the cold on Mahoney Playground by myself day and night. The people in the hood would walk by and shout, "You're crazy, it is too cold, and it will not help you." All those things and more. However, I was determined to be good like my friends silk and worm who were two of the best basketball players in New York city from The Rock (Mahoney Playground) Jersey Street New Brighton. In New York, the best ballplayer, the best dressed, the most popular, the best-looking, the wavy haired—these were the guys who were getting all the girls, but of course, I didn't fall into any of the categories mentioned, so I had to devise a plan. If I wanted these pretty girls, I had better get started. The first thing was to learn how to play ball and get my hair wavy. I wanted my hair wavy, but my mother kept telling me that my hair would always be nappy, and she'd ask why I was carrying a brush around. All I said to myself was, *I'll show you.* I knew what kind of girls I wanted, so I ignored my mother's remarks. One day, I went to the barber, got my hair cut, and asked the barber how to do it, so after the shop closed, he showed me systematically. So now my hair has been wavy for thirty-five years, no thanks to my mother. Therefore, the lesson I am teaching is that be determined no matter what it takes.

I got tired of my father hitting my mother, causing black eyes, and forcing her to wear dark shades, so I asked to go to camp. When I got there, I saw that they had a bunch of activities indoors and outdoors. I started to box. There were two purposes for this—one was to stop people from picking on me and the other was to protect my mother from my father. After the second summer at camp, when I came home in September, I vowed that my father will never hit my mother again, and when he attempted to, I told him, "Do not do it." Enough was enough. Men were not supposed to hit women no matter what. Since my hands were good, all the mother beatings, kids picking on me, name-calling, all that stopped. At last, I was king and running things, no more bullying me around. I started hanging in the streets. My mother did not want me to, but my stepfather at the time, KC (mom's second husband), convinced my mother to let me hang out late on weekends, stating, "He is the oldest, and he has to learn how to handle himself on the streets." So late night New York, here I come (green). First, party in Park Hill, Staten Island, New York. Party ends at 2:30 a.m. I call Mom, letting her know where I am, so she said, "Take a cab with some hood friends, home to Jersey Street Projects." Therefore, I got in the cab and sat in the back in the middle (wrong green). Mom is waiting outside the building for cab to arrive. Cab arrived. Because I am green and did not know where to sit when the cab pulled up to the building, everyone jumped out and left me sitting. Mom said, "It is your fault. Pay the taxi. Learn the streets."

In our household, our father did not allow no soda, no candy, and no gum. Wash your hands before eating, grace before eating. No talking while eating, and we could not drink fluids until after all our food was eaten. Don't try to sneak; it will cost you in the way of a slap. We never wanted for anything even after my mother divorced my biological father. Our father always told us, if we need something, to find him and he would give it to us. In addition, if you stole or robbed anyone to get money and get in trouble, he would never hear of that. That is why I have never been to jail except for traffic violations. In addition, I tell my kids the same thing. My father used to take me over the women's houses. I knew what he was doing in the back room. I was trying to get the woman's daughters. Everybody's going to have some fun around here.

As for our babysitter L and S, Mom thought they were good babysitters. They were a little older than I was, but since my joint was big when I was young, the babysitters wanted to have sex with me. (I learned early.) The best babysitters you ever wanted and pretty too. Mom never knew. Ha ha! When she said they were babysitting, I could not wait.

My mother was cheap; she said she never had any money. Boy, that had me mad. I used to say we had no more or no less than anyone else. "Why do you never have any money?" I got to the point I told my mother, "When you get some money, let me know." Yeah, that bad. She would always say, "Go ask you father," and I did. Thank God for good father, or I would have been a criminal if it were not for my father. God bless his soul.

In New York, the gangs that existed back then were the Savage Skulls and the Black Spades. You automatically knew who it was by the emblems and colors or their jean jackets, which by the way were turned inside out at night and back to normal during the day.

I played ball in winter at a place called Cromwell Gym, one of the biggest gymnasiums in New York, about a fifteen-minute walk from my house. During the week, I had to be in the house at 11:30 p.m. and 3:00 a.m. on the weekends. At fifteen, I started drinking beer and smoking weed. It was malt liquor called Olde English 800—we called it 800. My parents didn't condone marijuana but told us, "If you're going to smoke, do it in the house to avoid police and stay out of trouble." During school, I never brought home books as for homework, nah! I did all schoolwork in school. Home is fun time.

When I graduated from junior high school, we had a big party. That is when it all began—sex, drugs, and style. My first stepfather was allowing me to stay out later, so that was the good side, but one time he tried to bully me too by sticking my fingers together with crazy glue and pushing me in a hot tub of water with all my clothes on. It just made me tougher. After a while, he could not do anything with me either. My hands were too good. Don't get me wrong; I didn't disrespect my mother or fathers, but I realized that sometimes they were hitting me when I hadn't done anything wrong. That had to stop. I did not mind getting a whooping if I was wrong, but if I am right, I did not let them hit me. Hold these hands, duck, weave, or run. In my hood, the person with the best hands was the king (me).

Well, my best friend, Monkey Man, was truly the best. Nobody messed with him or me. The whole hood was scared of him except me. My biological father drank Johnnie Walker Red and smoked Pall Mall cigarettes, which both contributed to his demise. Due to this causing my father's death, I do not drink or smoke since he died. I feel better since I stopped and saved money.

My first stepfather worked in a prison at the Lorton Reformatory in Lorton, Virginia, which has since closed. I used to stay up every night so I could talk to him about the happenings in the penitentiary. He was the one also who prepared me for going to prison by the horror stories and letting me go to the prison with him sometimes to pick up his check. Now is the story about how we got to Virginia in the first place. His first job site was Lorton Reformatory, so that means we had to move to Virginia. In the meantime, while my father was trying to find a house for us in Virginia, he was commuting back and forth from Virginia to New York City on the weekends to see Mom. One weekend, he came home, and my sister Lisa saw one of the hood boys robbing a lady's house down the hallway, so she came back to tell my stepfather, and of course, he hyped up just out of training with handcuffs. He ran down the stairs and questioned the man, and the man said, yes, he robbed the woman's house. My stepfather arrested him and called the police. He was charged with breaking and entering and burglary, and got eight years. Now that same night, one of the brothers came to our house. They called him Black Joe. When he came to the door, he asked my mother, "Why did your daughter Lisa tell on my brother he was only robbing a white person?" My mother said, "After you finish robbing white people, who is next?" So he stated, "We are going to kill your kids." My mother, only four feet eleven inches, told him to hold the door for a minute and calmly walked to the cabinet under the kitchen sink to get the meat cleaver and ran back to the door, attempting to chop that man up. At first, I was scared when the man came to the door, but after I saw that my mother was going to risk her life to protect ours, I was scared no more. The shit was on. So of course, my stepfather's weekend visit was over, so now it was just me and my mother and sisters. The family we were up against had thirteen brothers and sisters. Since we knew the threat was real, our mother asked us the next morning if we were going to school. We were moving soon, so it would not be long. My sisters declined, but I still went every day because I felt if anybody were going to be killed, it would be me. I would not let you hurt my mother or sisters. I had to walk my mother every day to the bus step and pick her up. They would knock out the lights in the hallway so they could attack us. During this time, I got jumped numerous times, shot at, stabbed, hit in the face with a brick—you name it, they tried it. I was only seventeen. This went on for a couple of months until we moved, but nothing happened to my family. The agreement that was made was when you returned to New York and left wherever we live at was to take me back to where my family was. When we got to Virginia, I attended Garfield Senior High School, played basketball, and went back one year so I could play. I got a chance to go to basketball camp in Buies Creek, North Carolina, and learned basic ball. It added to my street game. We wound up winning the state championship the next year. During one game against DeMatha, I hit fifty points, and we lost. The coach told me in the locker room, "Too bad, you should have hit fifty-two. You might have won." I felt good than bad. During that time, the ball players had all the girls. My girlfriend at the time was half black and Chinese. Boy she was fine. My mother and father loved her. I cannot say that about her mother and father about me. I got my first car when I was in high school. It was a Ford Pinto. I also had my first son in the back seat by a white girl T. The oldest son is named David. She would not have an abortion because she was Mormon. She moved away while she was pregnant. I did not see my son until I got a job at FBI Headquarters. She got a job soon after I did and brought him to the job to see me. He was very light-skinned, of course.

Drugs and Alcohol

I started smoking weed when I was thirteen or fourteen years old; everyone was doing it. We were drinking Olde English 800. I was doing that until eighteen, and then I started drinking Long Island Iced Tea (wrong). Alcohol is an addiction. You think you feel good, but all it does is make you feel off balance and talk stupid, fight, and cause car accidents. I watched drug addicts in New York City have seizures, vomit, and concussions. I tried coke powder (cocaine) around twenty and sprinkled it on weed or snorted it. Around twenty-five, here comes crack. At first, I sprinkled it on weed and smoked it like that, thinking that I was not going to be hooked just because I was putting it on weed. Little did I know what was to come. Then I started selling powder so I could have some and make money too. Next thing you know, I was my best customer. I started cooking powder into rock form then breaking it up and putting that on weed. Next thing, I was smoking pure rock and a lot of it. I didn't mind spending the money as long as somebody else goes to purchase it, but with that comes people undermining you because of the addiction, telling stories, like "I lost it," "Somebody stole it," "This is all they gave me," knowing they were lying because of the addiction. I was a payday crack addict—only on payday before I ate, paid bills, brought groceries, anything. Sometimes I never came home until three or four days later, broke as shit, looking crazy, smelly, had not eaten or showered. I tell people crack is an addiction.

Drug Experience 1:
I had a friend named Wayne. We all used to go over to his house to smoke. He had no job, no money, but he smoked so we knew we could go over his house to smoke free. Almost (by that, I mean the house always gets a hit first). When you smoke crack in a bowl, a film adheres to the glass. That is called residue. The only way to get that out is grain alcohol. Remember, alcohol of that nature is for external use only, so since I knew that, I never smoked residue. Everyone doesn't feel the same way. For instance, every time we smoke a little bit, Wayne wanted to clean the bowl, which meant pouring alcohol into the bowl, swishing it around, and pouring it into a glass mirror, then lighting it and letting it dry. Then you take a spoon (round part) and smear it all around the mirror until it dries. After that you then take a razor and scrape the mirror resulting in crack cocaine. I never smoked residue. I had a cut card even when smoking crack. No residue. No prostitutes.

Drug Experience 2:
I lived in an apartment building called 900 Park Terrace on Wheeler Road in southeast Washington, DC. At that time, that building was Crack City. They were selling, buying, and using everything almost

on every floor. Let me show you how treacherous it was, the crack trade. I used to mess with this girl on the ninth floor. She was a crack head. I would often go up to her house to smoke or purchase crack. One afternoon, I went up to her house to purchase two working fifties. This means you could sell some and smoke some. "I blessed everyone" is street slang for giving everyone some of one of the fifties. This means I had one 50 left, so I put that away for a later date or later on. Now everyone is finished and geeking for more, so now I am about to leave. She says "New York, I know you have one left." I say "Nah!" At this time, I could hear a loud man talking at the elevator. She opened the door and stated that it is the police at the elevator. I was the only one in here with something to lose so if I do not share the other fifty, she was going to call the police on me. Never went back up there no more. The addiction. One time before that, I was up to her house, smoking and drinking. Then there was a loud knock at her door. We were already paranoid, so she opened the door, and this young boy was at the door, holding his head. He stated that someone had hit him in the head with a bat; he was bleeding profusely. All he said was, "Can I get a hit of crack?" I said "Please give that man a hit." The addiction—it got so bad in that building that the drug dogs were brought in to sniff at apartment doors. Alcohol—I used to drink to the point where I could not function, drive, or walk. As a result, I have been involved in two serious car accidents.

One accident was on June 10, 1996; I hit a telephone pole and tore up my BMW 633 CSI, which probably saved my life. I was at the Classics Restaurant, and it was a hurricane named Bertha that went through the city. I could not see due to the weather. The car was a total loss. I lost a tooth and had five hundred stitches. I had broken my left foot and had eighty stitches in the right side of my face. I was out of work one year because of this accident. It was only by the grace of God that I survived. You would have thought I would have stopped drinking then. I did not. I was in the hospital for a while. After all was said, I had five surgeries to put me back together.

When you are on drugs, you forget about everything, but I did not. I tried to keep a low profile and away from everything and everyone. On this night, I had been smoking crack all day, and I had to work that night. I was fine on the way to work, but when I got through the turnstiles, I became hostile, cussing people, taking trash, just crazy disobedient. At one point, I saw the floor manager walking around, and at that time, the management was mean, especially to new employees, so I got mad and started to try to find the manager to beat up. Drugs and alcohol make you crazy. Here I go, trying to find the manager, with no shirt on, chest sticking out, drunk, belligerent, and if I keep going, I was getting ready to be fired. Therefore, E. Kendall grabbed me and made me a bed so I could sleep it off. The next day, I had to apologize to my coworkers and supervisors. I was also drinking E & J Liquor.

Childhood:
This is how this works when my mother and father's job transferred back to New York. I was in the twelfth grade. She went home to get a place to live. When she found one, she came down with my favorite cousin Gerald K Williams aka Gee Money, to drive the U-Haul back. I had helped my mother load the U-Haul. After we were finished, my dear mother informed me that I was not going back to New York with her. I was shocked to see that my dear mother had just told me that they had gotten place to live in New York and didn't get enough room for me so I couldn't go after we made the agreement before we left New York that if they went back they would take me back where my family was.

Drugs Experience 3:
I had just gotten married (still on crack, mind you). One Saturday night, I decided to hang out on Bruce Place, southeast (how ironic), of course, to smoke crack. I started out with three hundred. At the time, I was driving a 320 I BMW. I started buying fifties and smoking with the people in the apartment, and eventually I ran out of money. So of course, we started geeking (looking for who was going to supply the next hit), no more money. At this time, two teenagers knocked on the woman's door. She let them in. They were supposed to be crack dealers. (Hey, right on time, but no money.) One of them, said, "If you ride as around, we'd give you some crack." So of course

(still geeking), I rode them around first to a fast food carryout, then home. Before they left, they blessed me with a piece. So of course, I was happy. Yeah, so I went back to the same people's house I just left to smoke with them. Of course, you have to bless the house woman. I put a piece in the pipe. It turned out to be soap. Party over. So I went home for the night (still geeking), waking the next day still geeking. I got some more money to go back to the same house I just left the night before, on Bruce Place, Southeast, DC, same people's house, to start smoking again. I ran out of money again. Guess who knocked on the door again. The same two young boys who beat me the night before. I confronted them and told them to straighten me up. So they gave me a twenty-piece. I was happy. I blessed the house woman again. Later, the two young boys who gave me that twenty told me they wanted their money or they were going to take my BMW. I told them I did not have any money, and they started attacking me and throwing stuff all around the woman's house and trying to take my keys. So the woman of the house told me to give her my keys, but I did not know her either, so I fought for a while, then she kicked the two boys outside. So now, they were waiting for me to come outside so they could take my BMW. I tried to get some people over in the neighborhood, but only one person helped for a while. At first, they did not believe it was mine, so like a fool, I was outside trying to go in my glove compartment while sitting in the passenger side. In the meantime, one of the young boys went around on the driver's side, opened the door, jumped in, and kicked the dashboard radio out. At the same time, the other young boy jumped on the hood and threw a brick through the window while neighborhood people were shooting at me while I tried to slide over, start the car, and get away while they were shooting. I went home and tried to hide my car with bashed-in windows from the wife and still tried to smoke more crack the same night. It is a beast. Barely survived death and still wanted a hit.

When I got the job at the Washington, DC, Post Office in 1987, I was still on drugs (smoking crack cocaine) by now, so life was still off balance. I had a 5.0 Mustang and lived in Marbury Plaza in Southeast, DC, on Good Hope Road with and old girlfriend, still smoking. Eventually, she put me out, so I was homeless now. I had a job and car, but nowhere to live. (It happened to the best of us. When you are living and doing the wrong thing, wrong things happen.) So now I was homeless. I still had a girlfriend who lived with her grandmother, so I could not stay there. She would bring me food and water so I could wash up with at the Exxon gas station on Pennsylvania and Alabama Avenue southeast. Imagine trying to wash up at the gas station with the floor dirty and bathroom nasty, but this is what drugs do to you if you let it. I called my family in New York. My mother stated, "You are all the way down there. How can I help you?" My family never helped at all, so little did I know it was God carrying me all the way. I slept in my car for three months—October, November, and December. Then finally, I moved into a crack house. I needed somewhere to stay. It was not the best-kept house, but nevertheless, they smoked a lot of crack in the house, and they tried to let me sleep in spite of the situation, knowing I worked midnights. I could not believe I was living in a crack house and the only one with a job. That is when I met my wife. She was a blessing in disguise. I have to honestly say that if I had not met her, no telling where I would be today. I tried to get out of the wedding because I knew I smoked crack, but she did not know and would not let me. Therefore, I was married and still wanted to smoke. (Not a good combination. Drugs and marriage do not mix.) Homeless and living in a car means no rest in the middle of the night. That is how I got constipation, and to this day, I still have not being able to go to the bathroom at nighttime. Imagine trying to wash up in the Amoco gas station with everybody watching me as if I were crazy. Crack had me so bad that when I did not have any money, I was selling air fresheners, two for a dollar (what ridiculousness).

When you sit around a smoke crack for a long period of time and you run out, you start freaking for the drugs or geeking, which means trying to find a way to get more or imagining you dropped some and stand looking on the ground or plucking people's carpets up, thinking you see a rock on the rug. You know damn well you did not drop a crumb, so stop plucking people's carpet up. In addition, you look like a fool. It also made me paranoid, so I always watched the door and try to smoke at the same time (doesn't work). Police knocked down your door, seizing your drugs. Either way, you lose, so don't smoke crack at all.

Rehabilitation

After my wife found out that I smoked crack (by the way, you won't be able to hide it from your loved ones—for example, my wife, girlfriend, mother, and sisters), she insisted that I go to a rehabilitation center. I went to talk to the woman at some rehab place on Wisconsin Avenue, Northwest, DC. When you first get there, you have to talk to a counselor before they admit you. Therefore, she started asking me questions about my life, school, job, possessions, goals, history. Once I explained all the stuff—that I did go to school, had good job, nice cars, nice women—the counselor would not admit me to the rehab center. Instead, he told me that since I already knew what the good life is and because crack was not the highlight of my life and I did other positive things, I have to get my ass back out there and do the right thing. He said this was not a place for me and that it was a place for those who only knew crack cocaine and did nothing else. So imagine me going back home to tell my wife that they would not admit me. Of course, she did not believe me, but it was true. Shortly thereafter, I was baptized, and slowly but surely, I got myself together and asked God to help me rid myself of this demon, and he finally did just before my youngest son was born. However, I tell people for a fact that not all the rehab clinics in the world will help you if you do not want to stop within yourself. I have seen people go to clinics for years and come out and soon as they got around the corner look for a hit of crack cocaine. Therefore, what I am saying is that you have to want it yourself, and remember the better things in life—to come away crack-free. My ex-wife really didn't help in the drug rehab process, so if you're married, don't talk negative about your spouse or loved one who may be suffering from an addiction but rather try to help if you really love and care about their well-being because it could just as well be you would you want your loved one to turn their back on you. Treat other as you would want them to treat you. When I was baptized, the water was so cold I thought Jesus was in the water. However, I thank God for everything because unbeknownst to me he was there all the time.

Women

I had three real girlfriends in thirty years and hundreds of others. That is why I am not married to this day. First was A. David, a white girl, short, dark-skinned, and fat to death. She was cute as a button but crazy as hell. One incident in our relationship, I was supposed to pick her up and take her to look for some furniture, but of course, I forgot, trying to hang out with these other girls I met. I picked the other girl up after work and brought her to my house and cooked some fish for myself my girl and her girlfriend finish eating a fish dinner. I cleaned up and took the trash out because it was fish. When I came back in, I forgot to lock the front door in a hurry to get some booty. I forgot about my real girl, which I was supposed to take furniture shopping. The other girl named C. Baker and I went in the back to knock boots. Meanwhile, the girlfriend was in the living room, watching television. I heard a knock on the door. Remember, I was having sex and on top of this girl when the knock came. Then I heard the front door open and close, and I heard feet running. Next thing I knew, my room door opened. It was my real girlfriend standing over me with a knife in her hand, getting ready to stab me. Remember I was buck naked, and so was the girl. She ran out the door to leave me to handle my girlfriend alone. She was digging the knife in my left hand, so I grabbed her wrists, and we had a tussle. I threw her out of the house, but before I got her out, not only did she stab me, she kicked me in the balls. I had her outside the door; she was banging to get back in, so I went to the bathroom to piss. That was when I saw blood come out. I went to the door and snatched her ass back in the house, picked her up, and slammed her on the ground. This was the first and last time I hit a woman. However, the booty was the bomb, and she looked gorgeous.

Job

Everyone hears about going postal. Well, let me explain what I have seen in my first two years. Years ago, most employees drank or drugged, so the whole place was a trip. Then you have your ten-point vets. So among alcoholics, drug addicts, war vets, and plain disgruntled employees, the place was a war zone. I, I, and I got into fights every day with anyone who thought they could fight or did not like me because I came from New York. I have always had a problem with that wherever I go. When I started with the government in 1981, at DOJ, I ran into girls from all over the United States. FBI Headquarters hired new EODs from all over the United States, except Washington, DC. Therefore, I started meeting girls from every state in the United States. Now you talk about some fine girls. Lord, I was going crazy. I think the building had 10,000 employees, and 7,500 were women. Boy, that was heaven. At first, I started as a fingerprint card assembler, which means we had to put the new fingerprint card with the old cards, and we were on production. I think it was 55 copies a minute. I hated that. After a couple of months, they moved me to the mail room, where I slept when I first came to work. My SAC (special agent in charge) was Mr. M. He trusted me.

Each morning, he would call down to the mail room to send for me so I could run errands and do different tasks. The supervisor in the mail room didn't like it. When he called for me they would always say, "Your father wants you." SAC, even though he was white, it did not matter to me. He was respectful and a nice man. I have never been prejudiced unless you did something to me. Mr. M and I worked out fine. I soon found out why he catered to me. First, we both came from Staten Island or Grimes Hill, so he checked my background. Ha! He treated me to breakfast and lunch. He was just a nice, down-to-earth man. Once I got in good with him, I felt he could get me another job (higher grade). I saw a security job on the board. I asked him about it (after all I was only a GSII). I had to get some money somehow, so he told me to fill out an application before the deadline and turn it in. I did about ten applications just to make sure. Mr. M said he knew the SAC of security, so he would put a good word in. I said thank you. I kept turning the application in but no response. Mr. M asked me, "Did you turn the application in?" I told him yes. I turned them in to the front office.

Once again, he asked me about the application. I told him that I made copies and turned them in personally to the front office. So now, we have to track them down because security unit did not receive my application yet. First, he told me if I were lying, I would lose my job. I took him to the front office, and the clerk told him, "Yes he turned a couple of applications in." Then Mr. M got mad. He talked to the secretary that if he found out that someone in that office was throwing away applications, he would fire them right on the spot. Eventually, my application found. It was way down to security, and I got the job, GS 5–9. He helped me get ahead. So do not be prejudiced of anyone. First, find out for yourself who they are before making judgments. When I got that job, I had access to the whole building, so now the women came in and out. I know women from almost every state in the United States. They used to ask, "Jones, you hit on so many women. Don't you get cursed out?" I replied, "Yeah, but I get a lot of booty too." Therefore, I tell people, in anything in life, the more you do, the law of average wins with anything.

Sex

Well, I remember when I first started at DOJ; I was sitting in the break room one morning, trying to get over a hangover. I think I was about nineteen or twenty. I was pretending to be asleep when I overheard the older ladies on the other side of the break room talking about their sexual partners and they were talking bad about them. I realized I didn't want anyone to talk about me like that, so I had to figure out a plan. I wouldn't be a bum in bed and have ladies talking about me. Therefore, I went to the bookstore and got a bunch of sex books so I could learn what to do, when to do it, and how to do it. Once I got there and read them, all I needed to do was get some specimen to practice on. I can honestly say that I do not personally know brothers who have had nicer, prettier girls than me. Most people wish they even knew the ones I knew. That is why I am not married, because when you have seen the best, forget about the rest. You cannot give me anything. I tell women, "If you do not like the way you look in the mirror, how do you expect me to?" Women want men to look good, and they look like anything. I can tell you that when you get married, make sure this is the one you could live with so you do not have to cheat.

Job (Words of Wisdom)

Association-Simulation means simply people who spend time should be doing the same thing. My father always told me when I was a youngster that you only have one or two friends. Pay homage to all those who were around you and those who mattered to you. For you, young people, my father always told me that you only need a few friends. I said friends, not associates, because the ones that you think are your friends won't be there in times of need. So keep your frequent hangout friends to one or two. Make sure that you all are doing the same thing—good things. I mean a job, school, sports, whatever your extracurricular activities are. They should have the same interests. For me, I have been having since I've been with the United States Postal Service. I have supportive friends who are there when I need them. The other two are also supportive and have been like brothers since I was at the FBI headquarters in 1981. These two brothers were actually my roommates, so they were like family. One came from St. Louis. He later retired as a Fairfax county polygraph detective. The other one came from Lexington, Kentucky, and retired as a Capitol Hill police sergeant. One thing is that the friends you have around you, your close friends, have a lot of influence and relevance to your decision-making, and the choices you make directly have an impact on your life's successes or failures. So I say, choose our friends wisely. Always remember you can choose your friends but not your family. You are stuck with them, and you can still handle them with a small handle spoon.

Remember the kind of friends you hang out with or fail to hang out with. You are with them, and they get in trouble. Because you are with them, even though you may have done nothing, you will get in the same trouble or predicament they are in. Don't get caught with these kinds of friends. They could hinder your success, and when you get in trouble, I'll be saying what my father told me about too many friends. He always said, "I already told you that hanging with the wrong people would get you trouble." He said, "Who is the fool, me or you?" I never wanted to be a fool in my father's eyes, so I kept my friends and associated to a minimum. Please listen to your parents. You may not see it then when you are young, but later on, when you grow up, you will understand. Always be wary of those trying to befriend you. Seek out ulterior motives, if any, or are they your genuine friends? Hopefully, you will be able to tell. Friends must be fair, supportive, real, truthful, and helpful. Most of all, be a good listener with some ideas and morals.

Rules to Abide by to Succeed

Don't forget, good people or friends always try to do the right thing and live a good life. These are the type of people you must have in your life.

Remember, no mortal is perfect, not even Jesus Christ, but he was pretty close.

Karma—what goes around comes around. That means if you live life less than exemplary and do things to people just because you can and being mean for no reason at all to mankind and others, you reap what you sow. So don't cause any harm to yourself or other family members just because you live and treat people mean for no reason at all and watch how fast it comes back to bite you in the ass.

My older friend from the FBI, Asst. ASAC W.M., told me when I started at FBI Headquarter, "Young man, a penny saved is a penny earned." This means if you save your money when you are able, it will always come in handy when you need to.

THE BOTTOM LINE

Religion. Believe in God. Remember without him, we are nothing. Believe it. With him, all things are possible, regardless of what humans tell you.

Hard times and despair. Like my old friends used to tell me, "Remember, think positive. Your cup is always half full instead of half empty."

Chores and tasks. Never put off chores or task until tomorrow if you can do it today. Make life a lot easier on yourself.

Purchasing anything. If it's not the best when it's brand new, how will it perform old? So sometimes, it's best to pay your money at first so as not to keep fixing or repairing it.

Determination. Never, never quit and let anything stop you. Sacrifice what you have to in order to get where you have to go. I call it putting on horse blinder or straight ahead. Determination is most important when you set any goal. This means that at all cost, you will not quit to achieve whatever your goal is. That means you must make whatever sacrifices needed to succeed, and do not quit no matter what. Stay focused on the task at hand. The only thing that should stop you is obvious. Go and get whatever it is to be had. No mortal should stop you.

Doing the right thing. I told my kids, "If you do the right thing, nine out ten times, the right thing will happen for you. Just the same if you do the wrong thing, ten out of ten times, the wrong thing will happen." So what I'm saying is, the *bottom line*, do the right thing, that's all.

Family. Protect your family. Mind your business. Help thy neighbors.

Driving (aggressive, fast, reckless). I've learned that in most places we go, we've been there before, and sooner or later, we will be going there again. So why go speeding and misleading, causing harm to yourself or another? Slow down. If you continue your behavior, you will sooner or later have an accident unnecessarily by going somewhere you've been before.

Diet. You must get plenty of rest. Drink plenty of water. Eat a balanced diet—meat and vegetables. Stretch. Be sure to include green leafy vegetables because most meat you consume is already dead.

After Diet Facial Wrinkles Aging-After you do all of the above in the beauty books I read it is said that it takes two muscles to smile and fifty to frown so first of all try to smile more than you frown so as not to wrinkle your face as much plus smiling and laughter helps you live longer then after all that do facial stretching exercises to keep your skin tight and looking younger for as long as possible research the beauty books to see what works for you.

Life's challenges. Always remember, God is never gone or give you more than you can handle. God is in charge, regardless of whether you do the right or wrong thing. So do the right thing. That's the bottom line. Don't sweat it. Pray.

Life skills and education. No matter who you are, if you go through life and just take a job, that's fine, but if you never learned a trade or get a degree or some form of skills of your own liking as far as education purposes, if you put nothing in your mind, people are not obligated to pay you anything. They will give you a mop or spatula just because you have no skill. So learn something at all cost. They can take everything away—your house, your car, all your worldly possession—but they can't take away your knowledge. Thank God.

Teenagers and adults, to achieve success, you must be amicable and more receptive to lessons learned. Listen to suggestions and advice by those older and more experience than yourself in order to avoid common mistakes.

THE BOTTOM LINE

"I can't." This is for fools. There is no such thing. If you pray, it will be done. When you say "I can't," you have defeated before you even try. First, try. You never will know if you don't give it your best shot.

Relationship/marriage (girlfriend/boyfriend/significant other). I never—and I mean never—messed with someone else's husband or wife or anything of the like. Avoid bad situations or harm to oneself or someone else. Do not be in a situation that you shouldn't be involved with in the first place. So make life safer for you and your family. And that's the bottom line.

Decision-making. Stand for the right thing and believe what you stand for, or else you will fall for anything. Don't let people tell you any old thing. Stick to your beliefs. Stand for something, or fall for anything. Don't be a fool.

Wearing your pants in this manner is very disrespectful. Teenager or young men, please pull your pants up on your butts and use a belt. That's what holes are for. No one wants to see your drawers or your ass. And you shouldn't want them to see it either. Leave that stuff in prisons and jails, where it comes from and where they are doing the peanut butter. You don't want to do that either.

Tattoos. Young people keep tattoos hidden, especially from the face, neck, and any place a job interviewer can see them so you will have a fair chance in getting a job or being successful, which you should want to be. It also messes your skin up for life. After tattoos remember when you get tats you can't give blood for the rest of your life not even to family members who might need it so think before you ink.

Young men dating women and exchanging numbers. The problem I was having was that I met women and we exchange numbers. I would call them a day or two later. For some reason, I would always get an excuse or something like that. I would be disappointed, which really knocked my spirits down. So I came up with a plan. I said, "From now on, when I meet women, I would only give my number," and I found out it was better. You know that your chances were good using that method. It worked all day. No more disappointments. When they called, it was on like popcorn because you knew they were interested in you.

There will be no malice in your heart. Live malice-free. Life will be more successful.

Remember, like my mother used to say, clothing, hairstyle, shoes, etc. makes you no better than anyone and no on smarter than you. And clothes don't make the person.

One of the most important aspects of success is planning. So always remember if you fail to plan, plan to fail, which clearly means one must always have some kind of plan. Hopefully a successful one, but nevertheless, one must go to sleep and wake up with a positive and successful plan that will enable you to live a healthy and prosperous life, which one should want for themselves and family.

Young adults' success in jobs, schools, and any endeavor. Be on time, especially to your place of employment and in starting your first job. Be there before time, not on time, and be what we call regular in attendance. In other words, go to work, do your work, and most importantly, learn your job well and not worry about what your coworkers do. Be responsible for your well-done job only.

The bottom line, young people, is please at least listen to and take advice from hard-working people who are more successful than yourself, but the most important thing is to listen and apply it to your life as needed. Please don't be stubborn and hard-headed for no darn reason at all because I found out that some of the advice was actually useful and worked. So at least listen because as one of my old bosses at the FBI Headquarters said, "Young man, nobody knows everything, and you will never know everything, so please listen."

When I was a young boy, I would watch my grandmother cook in the kitchen, and while waiting for those homemade rolls to rise before she put them in the oven, she used to always tell me, "Grandson, idle time is the devil's mind," which meant if you are doing nothing productive or positive, then this allows the negative and bad ideas and actions to come into play, so stay positive and productive, and keep the devil out of the way of your lifes success.

Personal conduct. Now about running your mouth, if you have nothing good or positive to say, sometimes it's best to say nothing at all, and remember, loose lips sink ships, and once those words come out, you can't take them back, so as my father taught me as far as that is concerned, keep your eyes and ears open and your mouth shut. You'll be surprised at what you might learn.

Personal hygiene (men showering). When you get older and take a shower, unless you have a real dirty job or just get that dirty, I learned that you can wash your body with your hand, which in turn will keep your body smooth as silk, so when a woman touch and feel you, your body won't be rough. I used this technique for forty years, and it works. To keep facial skin smooth wash with your hands it works ive done it for forty years.

Investing in oneself. In New York, they have saying that goes, "Scared money won't make any money," which clearly means if you aren't willing to spend some money in something legitimate for you and your family, which will possibly reap lifetime dividend, you don't deserve the rewards. Don't let anyone deter you about making an investment that could lead to big money for you and your family. For instance, when I mention to people I was going to pay to have a book published, everyone said they wouldn't do it along with a lot of negative things. That's when I thought about scared money. I said God gave me the chance or shot to make unlimited money. The moral of this story is that sometimes you have to take chances with the opportunity God has given you so you and your family can be well-off. Watch for the advice, especially if they are not trying to get paid. Remember, it's your life and money. Watch for the jealous and envious characters. Remember, it's your well-being at stake.

Law of averages. This means that from a success point of view, the more you try something—be it getting a better job, making more money, or my favorite pastime, trying to date those pretty fine women—the more chances that you will be successful and achieve your goal. I'll give you two examples. First one is concerning a job. I was working at the FBI Headquarters as a security officer when I decided to attempt to get a better-paying job at another government agency. At first, I only put one or two applications in and didn't get any response, so then I thought about how I tried to date and talk to many women and how that worked. I did the same with the job search by putting in twenty-five applications, and soon, I got a better-paying job. What I'm saying is, the more, the better, and that's the bottom line. As with most, not all, it comes down to the law of averages.

Staten Island (the Rock) New Brighton: Domestic Violence (Beating Women)

When I was about seven or eight years old, inside the corner store on Jersey Street, New Brighton, Staten Island, New York, across the street from Mahoney playground, I was chasing this little girl that was teasing me. I was going to beat her down. All of a sudden, one of the older guys in the neighborhood grabbed me by the collar after seeing that I was going to hit this girl and stopped me. He asked me what I was doing. I told him I was going to beat her up. He told me that men weren't supposed to hit females. He specifically told me that young men need a woman. You might not need a man, but you need a woman, and boy, oh boy, he was right. I wouldn't want anyone beating on my sisters or any other female in my family. So from that day on, I never hit a woman, and soon after that, as I got older, I didn't let my father beat on my mother anymore. I always told my sisters' husbands and boyfriends, "Before you put your hands on any of my family members, send them home or you'll have to see me, no questions asked." That's the bottom line.

Women

In most of my relationships, it mostly goes well, no adultery. That is why I always ask when you meet someone. First question is, are they married? Second, do they have someone, so as not to get mixed up in the wrong situation that could cost you your life? I myself try to stay away from someone else's woman, but sometimes, unknowing to you, it happens.

For instance (remember, this never happened before), I met this pretty girl on the job. At first, I was not going to talk to her since she was a new employee. At first, I would go by and say a couple of words regarding the job. Let them in on the dos and don'ts. After a while, I stop going around and talking to her due to my workload. So consequently, all talk ceased. Therefore, I was riding by one day at work, and she was staring at me, and so was I. So finally I stopped, and she stated, "What is wrong with you?" (I did not sleep with you, because if I did, you would not be frowning.) It piqued my interest, so after that, the shit was on. Now I asked if she was married and had a man or whatever. She stated no. Therefore, we got together, and I knocked her boots. She was hooked; it is on. However, her naked body was not what I thought when she took her clothes off. She was all right but had double stomach and stretch marks. Here we go, another pretty face with what I called mismatched body—cute face with messed-up body (messed-up feet, hands, etc.) and vice versa. Women want you to be in good condition, but their body is messed up. The way I look at that is you only can ask for what you give. Ha ha! So now I was messing with this girl, thinking I was the man, but not really.

On this day, April 8, 2008, I was waiting for my supposedly girlfriend (who by the way always lies) to call me after she got out of school, helping her daughter in her class test. It was 12:30 p.m. but no call, so something tells me to take a shower, get dressed, and go over to her house. I did. When I got there, I noticed the same truck she had been sitting out in front her so-called kid's godfather's truck. Well, I knocked on the door, and what do you know? It was a man's voice, so I answered, "It's New York, Where is Mickey?" She opened the door with a robe on, and a little short baldheaded man stepped to the door, talking smack. I calmly said, "So this is how you live, then you wonder what is wrong with you and why you are having bad luck?" This was her real boyfriend that she never told me about. Therefore, I was a fool for the first time.

Streets

Well, in the streets, when you give respect, you get respect. Never take anything from anybody. Treat everyone fairly. Take no shit from no one, ever. I never did anything to anyone unless they deserved it. Be straight up, no bullshit. I don't sugarcoat anything; I will battle in a minute. I do not care how big you are. As the old saying goes, the bigger they are, the harder they fall.

Experience:
During one experience on the streets of DC, I was hustling up town one day when I was selling my wares when I approached some dudes I recognized, asking them if they were looking for such and such. They told me to hold on; they will get back with me in a minute. Fifteen minutes later, two guys came across the street with long coats on. The guy I talked to signaled to me to talk to those guys, so I went in an alley. That was when they pulled their guns out and started to stick me up, hitting me in the head with the butt of the gun, causing a big gash on top of my head, and you can still see the spot to this day. While they were robbing me, they were trying to handcuff me to a bar above me. That's when I really started to fight. I couldn't explain to police how and why I got handcuffed to the bar, so the fight was on, and of course, watch out for the long coats in the summertime.

Women

For me, since I did not have any family here, I depended on the girls I dated to be there for me since family abandoned me, and it worked. All you have to do is treat them right. You have to be a decent brother, meaning keep yourself up, keep a job, and recognize all holidays, birthdays, Valentine's Day, Mother's Day, and Christmas. Most of all, you have to satisfy them in bed, no exceptions.

Dating

I was dating Kay around the time, probably one of my first real girlfriends. When we first met, I told her my penis was around fifteen inches. She said she had bigger and that it was not anything, so we set a date up. On that date, she had told me she was coming off her period, and we could still have sex, so we did. After we finished, she was bleeding a little heavier than she should, so I told her to take a bath or shower, so she did. While she was in the bathroom, I kept checking on her. Noticing the water was getting redder and redder, I asked her what she thought was wrong. She did not know, so I gave her a towel to put between her legs and drove her to Hadley Memorial Hospital in Southwest, DC. On the way to the hospital, we agreed not to tell them we had sex (soon that would change). After getting to the hospital, she had lost so much blood that she started to go unconscious. The doctor came to ask me what happened to her (remember our agreement). I told him at first that I did not know. I guess he thought I either raped her or stuck something long up her vagina. Either way, since I was not talking, he was going to call the police. Therefore, I asked him, "Could I talk to my girlfriend before she went unconscious so she can tell the truth before I go to jail for just having sex?" After she told the doctor, we were fine, except for the nurses, who were looking at me as if I were crazy because my joint, being so long, broke her cervix, which I understand was hard to do. Therefore, I was a celebrity of sorts. Remember, this was the same woman that helped me while I was homeless and living in my car. She was a real sweetheart. I have seen her recently from a distance at the wharf in Southwest, DC, at the waterfront. She was still fine and pretty.

Women

I did not have hardly any male friends, mostly all female, so I learned the sex trade well. So well, I never had any cheating that I know of until a last one I fooled with (Mickey). All you have to do is satisfy them in all the ways, and you will not have to worry about adultery. First, make sure you get the kind of woman you do not have to cheat on. You will not know her personality; just make sure the body and looks are close to what you like, then work from there. I am not the best looking or the worst, but I have managed to have hundreds of girls throughout my lifetime in all shapes, colors, sizes, attitudes, drama, issues, etc. If you are going to have someone around, you let it be a woman. You do not need men around; you only need women. You really need two male friends, because the rest are not going to help anyway. It keeps you out of trouble. It was an advice I got from my father, and he was right. Too many male friends are unnecessary. The key is to keep pretty women around you. It will make you successful and keep you going ahead. There is only one thing I regret when I was younger, and I have to ask God for forgiveness because back in the days, no one used protection. I had gotten a couple of girls pregnant. Since we were young and not trying to have a family or baby, we had abortions. I always ask God for forgiveness. When my wife got pregnant, one would think that since we were married, she would have told me the news first but she did not. I found out from my mother. Ever since then, I wondered if marriage made a difference. At least I didn't make too much noise about it and voluntarily helped take care of my son, and I am proud of it and him. All I tell my kids is "Do the right thing, and I will help. If you do not, I will not help."

Religion

I truly believe that because of my belief in God, he always helped me even though I was not doing the right thing. I never took anything from anyone or treated anyone wrong. I believe that living like this truly kept me out of harm's way. For sure, without God, I would not be here today. So I say believe in God wholly and try to live right. Always remember that God is in control even when you think you are you are not. So live right.

Watch for the Setup

I had a woman experience back in 1982 to 1983 when I started working for FBI Headquarters. I lived on Holmes Place, Northwest, DC, off Park Road. It was a basement apartment with my own entrance. It was okay, but cold and damp. Kitchen facilities were not that great. However, it was a start. I had a Pontiac Sunbird. I brought it new, but I had the car before I got the basement apartment. I met this girl from southeast. She lived in Marbury Plaza apartments on the garden side. I started dating her, and I brought her to my house on occasion. So naturally, she knew where I lived. I did not have much; I had a thirteen-inch TV, portable radio, and a few clothes. It was already furnished with the basic stuff. At the same time, once I moved into the apartment, I had a dilemma somewhere to live or keep the car, so naturally I let the car go. However, I was up on my notes, the car, started knocking, and I only had it six months. I voluntarily turned the car in. So now, I had no car for a minute. In the meantime, I was still talking to this girl in SE. During this time, I was in a basketball league at the bureau with some coworkers who would later, unbeknownst to me, be my roommates. One night, before the game, this girl from SE called and asked what I was doing, so I told her I had a game at 8:00 p.m. I talked to her for a while before I went to the game. I took the bus down to the job for a game. After the game, Derek and Cornell, my coworkers and best friends, gave me a ride home since I didn't have a car. When we got to the house, I heard Derek say, "Sport, your door is wide open." I said, "What?" I got out the car only to find the property owner down there. The apartment was all ransacked, and my TV, clothes, etc. were gone. I figured that it was the girl because she was the only one who knew I was not going to be home. Therefore, she became a suspect.

Young men, first of all, when talking to a young lady, please talk and act like you have some sense, which means be well-mannered and respectful! After that, all you have to do is—like they taught me when I was a young boy on the Rock, Staten Island—keep making them laugh. LATWTTB (laugh all the way to the booty). Try it and see (guarantee). Be safe.

They also taught me when you, as we used to say, get a mack, a tongue-kiss, or kiss on the lips, you are supposed to get some booty also. Try that and see (guarantee). Be safe.

Always remember that's someone's daughter.

Young adults having children. First of all, try (but not always possible) to get some sort of education or trade skill so you can provide for yourself and your children. But most of all, get a good job with benefits. Always take care of your children because they didn't ask to be here. When you have kids, your life no longer belongs to you until they become adults. Not taking care of your children will directly result in bad luck, karma, and missing God's blessing.

Growing adults (18–21). First of all, if you raise your children with good morals and if you point them in the right direction, by the time they reach adult age, they should be prepared to do something productive. So I tell my children when you reach eighteen, you have two choices, and neither one of them is staying home. LOL.

Young men, in picking your women, this is how I choose my women. First of all, as a young man, you must have certain things. First thing is a good job for your own spot (place to live) and hopefully your own decent vehicle. After that, you must pick the type of woman you won't cheat on and you blend with (get along with). After that, make sure it's the kind of woman you won't mind helping, because as a man that is your job—to better the person you are with. Most of all, give your loved one truthful and sound advice, and if they have children, help with them because they didn't ask to be here. Always remember, getting the booty in any relationship is a no-brainer. I always wanted to be known for helping, telling them the truth and giving good sound advice, which goes a long way, and hopefully, you'll be truly respected. It will show that you weren't just after the booty and truly cared about the person and their family's well-being.

Remember, it's okay to help anyone, but never help yourself out of anything, because remember, you must be well-off to help really help someone in need. So to stay on top of your game, always keep yourself well-groomed and clean cut. Please keep your spot clean—your bathroom, kitchen, etc.

One of My Favorite Girlfriends: Loved One vs. Cancer

Shirlyn D. Heyward was one of my favorites, if not the best girlfriends I ever had. She was nice, sexy, and really fine. I met her on the job at the post office. She was so sexy. I had to talk to her because when I first saw her, I knew one thing if nothing else; I wouldn't have to cheat on her or at least by the way she looks. I started dating her, so as the years went on, of course, we fell in love, and I would have married her any day, but she was the caretaker for her son and elderly mother, who was bedridden. I told her it didn't make a difference to me. I dated her for thirteen years. One weekend, when she was over my house, I was feeling her breast and felt a small lump. She smoked cigarettes and had a history of breast cancer in her family, and one of her sisters had already passed from it. When I felt the lump (at that time we cried and hugged), she had to get a biopsy. At that time, the procedure was not covered by her health insurance, so I paid for the procedure, and they found a lump in her left breast, oh god.

So now of course there were some decisions to be made to save her life. First, take the lump out or remove the breast. I told her that if it would save her life, they need to remove the breast completely. She was having a hard time with that. She knows I'm a booty man. Her breasts were really small anyway, so as far as I'm concerned, they could go, especially if they save her life. She finally decided against removal of the breast and opted for lump removal, which in the end did not fare well. First of all, when a loved one has cancer, you must be there for them mentally, physically, spiritually, and have their best interest at heart, nothing else. I mean, yeah, I wanted to have sex, but it wasn't about me (throw it out of your mind). Also, make sure at least before you go to chemotherapy, to be able to get the meds. Your blood cell count must be good in order to even get the medicine. Her treatment was at Howard University Hospital. I took her to eat twice a week so her nutrition would be right so she could get the medicine (salad every time). Always be helpful in encouraging. They are already going through enough. The hardest part was watching the nurse stick in the needle in her hand, trying to find the vein, which most had collapsed, and it was hard to watch when they had to keep sticking and probing the back of her hand, trying to get the blood cell count. Many times, I wanted to trade my hand for hers when they could not find the vein. A couple of times, they had to get the blood from her foot. The sad part about the whole thing is after all the pain and the surgery, my lovely friend still passed. I did all I could do, including pray, but the Lord called her home. God bless her soul, RIP. I truly loved you. I couldn't stop tearing while writing this. That's how sad I still am. Life hasn't been the same since she left. Still not married sixteen years later. Just haven't seen someone like her. It is what it is. I am still waiting on God to send me the right one.

Another Favorite Girlfriend

Her initials are AH but we will call her REDS, because she was real light-skinned, tall, with long black hair. She was gorgeous (and still is, saw her recently). I met her at Hands Point in Potumac Park in Southwest, DC. At the time we met, she had ten kids with her, but I didn't care. She was fine. Like I tell you, young people, children didn't ask to be here. So I started talking to her, and before the day was over, we were kissing. This was the first woman I ever met and kissed on the first day and didn't even know her. I had come to find out later on that only two of the ten kids were actually hers. I dated her for about ten years and would have married her, but you know how things go. I loved her. God bless her and her family.

Childhood

While growing up on Staten Island in New York City, we lived in the Jersey Street Projects. It was always a challenge, and peer pressure was always there. You had to have the best clothes, best basketball game, best fighter, and the finest girls. The key here is not to worry about peer pressure and be the best you could at what you want and be determined and not to let others deter you from your goal, and remember, it will not always be this way. Your time will come eventually. Our father and mother were strict as hell. We could not have candy or soda. We could not drink our fluids before eating all our meal, or our face would be slapped. In New York City, you learned a lot from the older kids in the hood, like giving respect, getting respect, and minding your own business. When it doesn't concern you, words don't mean anything pertaining to people calling you out of your name. Do not respond to such actions, only when people put hands on you, then it is time to react with the same. Our grandmother, my father's mother, was our caretaker when we were young while our parents worked, so most of my living habits came from my grandmother, like ironing, grooming, treating others courteously, and protecting my sisters and myself. Grandma always told me, "If someone was picking on you and they were bigger than you, grab the biggest stick you can find and protect yourself." Grandmother says, "Never be afraid of anyone unless it is a bear." I hated when my mother and father were having a spat because normal stuff wasn't getting done, like weekly haircuts on Saturday morning. As a result, my mother was trying to cut my hair with scissors, which turned out to be horrendous haircut. I had to attend school like that, which caused me being made fun of. As I got older, I started to defy my mother. I would not let her cut my hair with scissors or perm in my sisters' hair, which was burning their hair out in bald patches, causing my sisters to be made fun of. It caused embarrassment for my sisters, and I had to protect them from other mean kids. I went to PS 31 Elementary School, IS 61 Junior High School, and Curtis High School on Staten Island, New York. The elementary and high school were within walking distance, and it was a ten-minute short bus ride to the junior high school. That summer, before going to high school, in those days, there was such a thing as freshman anxieties. The upper classmen would tell you all summer that in your first couple of weeks of school, you would be subjected to a physical beatdown because you're a new freshman. Some of the kids did not come to school the first couple of weeks to avoid the beatdown, but of course, I went and got beaten down every day for about two or three weeks, which included chasing in between classes, knocking books out of your hands. Of course, you are new to the school, so you have no sense of direction in a new school and have no idea of where your classes are. I was late every day for the first couple of weeks due to being a new freshman. I was glad that was over and could not wait for the next year's freshmen. Ha ha! This was a lasting experience that I will never forget, which made me stronger even though I was afraid at the beginning and all summer long, but at the end, it was worth it.

Cars

My first car while attending Garfield Senior High School was a Ford Pinto. My mother and stepfather insisted they bought for me. Ultimately, I wound up paying for myself, which helped me to be responsible, and it made me get a job to pay for insurance. By moving from New York City to Dumfries, Virginia, I started to learn in-depth about how cars work and how to work on them. That part of my life I wouldn't have learned in New York, being that there was mass transit and no need for cars like Dumfries, Virginia. At that time, there was no mass transit and way out in the boondocks. I started to take a liking to automobiles and started to read consumer reports for the best cars and fastest cars.

My second car was a Pontiac Sunbird, which I did not want to buy. Since my mother and father weren't trying to help me after getting a federal job, one of my stepfather's best friends, whom my parents left me with, was willing to cosign for me. At that time, I wanted a trans am, but he wouldn't cosign for that, so I wound up with a Pontiac Sunbird, which was brand new, with no miles. It was white, two doors, with brown interior. My car note was $189 per month, and my paycheck at that time at the FBI Headquarters was $179 biweekly, so you see, so you see I was barely surviving. I started driving back and forth to New York City while changing oil regularly and doing maintenance. I only had seven thousand miles when I found out that the engine was gone. I wrote the Pontiac Division, and they did not want to help. Therefore, this was the last little car I ever brought, and at this time, I had to choose between having a car or somewhere to live. Survival is most important.

At this time, I voluntarily turned the car in so I could pay rent instead of car note. Therefore, I tell young adults now that if you live at home, buy all the stuff you need to survive. Pay cash. That way, the only thing you have is rent and car insurance. You even save money today by paying cash for your car. My father used to say the only payment you should have is rent and car note, and if you can eliminate the car note, which I did for a long time by purchasing a dependable used car and pay cash for it. Remember, put your priorities in place—roof, food, and car.

After turning the car in, I saved my money and brought a 1969, 2002 BMW, which was an older model, but I had read that the ratings were strong, and I hope could withstand my foot on the pedal, and true to fact, I rode that car twenty-two times to and from New York City to DC in two years, and it never broke down on me. It never had no problems on the highway even at one hundred miles per hour, so this proved to me that the BMW was a truly a good motor car; hence, I started buying BMWs thereafter for a while.

I owned five BMWs, two Mercedes, and two Lexus. And of all the cars I owned, Lexus is the best as far as dependability, maintenance, performance, and durability. Before I bought these cars, I read the consumer report. The cars whose consumer report said wouldn't do good didn't do good. The ones like Lexus had exceptional consumer report, and it did very well in all the categories they said. So I'm saying that before you waste your money and be disappointed or downright mad, read the consumer report first before you purchase any item. This is the twenty-first century. You don't have to purchase items that just don't work good. Read the consumer report. It will save you thousands of dollars, especially young people. Most of you starting out don't have a lot of money as I did when I was a young adult, so read the consumer report.

My third car was a lime-green GLE Saab, which is a Swedish car. It is a four-cylinder front-wheel drive, because in Switzerland they have snow and mountain slopes that require front-wheel drive mobility to get around in these parts. It was comfortable but not much power, especially when turning on air conditioning. I would lose power especially on the highway. One thing I learned about cars at a young age is that if it isn't broken, don't mess with it. By that, I mean on the Saab. I overdid myself, tightening the transmission oil pan, which ended up stripping the bolt and causing the transmission to constantly leak, so I had to trade it in.

My fourth car was a Black Toyota Supra with the digital package. It was dependable, not agile but powerful for a V6. The digital package was colorful and exciting at night, but that engine failed due to lack of maintenance.

The fifth car was a Ford Mustang 5.0 V8, fast at that time. I was on crack cocaine, trying to deny I had a habit. I was still working but homeless, with all my belongings in the trunk riding around DC. With nowhere to go to call home when I purchased this car, I took over someone's note, but then I didn't pay the note or car insurance, so eventually they repossessed the car with all my belongings, and I never got them back. During this time, I was parking in front of people's houses, trying to sleep, and they were constantly calling the police, so I had to keep moving from house to house during the day. I went to the parks and washed up in the gas stations. On one occasion, I was riding on Minnesota Avenue, Southeast, DC, around twelve midnight when I was pulled over by DC police, but during the stop, a police officer was shot, so he left without checking my car thoroughly, in which I had a crack pipe and all the tools. So thank God again. After they repossessed that car, I was now homeless without a car. I stayed in Southeast, DC, off Alabama Avenue with some drug friends. Still employed but with no real home to say, I smoked crack all day and worked at night. I try all the time to keep my job and look presentable, but I was looking noticeably raggedy and disheveled. I was calling in all the time and was still a junior employee. My coworker Ed always gave me a ride to and from work unless he would be off, so basically, I was homeless with a job (it can happen to anyone), doing drugs. But by believing in God, I knew that if eventually I did the right thing, the right thing would happen.

While staying at my drug friend's apartment, of course, I knew people in the hood who fooled with crack, so getting to know them and me having a job was a perfect match, I thought. During this time, I took the metro to work while temporarily living with my friend and helping out with groceries and some bills. During this time, I met my wife whom I thought was religious because I met her going to her church.

My next car was a 1980 BMW 3201. It was just before I got married but still on crack. I think I paid $2,500 for it. I put alpine stereo and sheepskin seat covers in it. I took a trip to New York City for my mother to meet my wife.

Court Date (DWI)

Dates of incarceration were May 17, 2010 through June 14, 2010 (thirty days).

May 17, 2010 through May 31, 2010, I was locked down on intake unit for fifteen days, twenty-four hours a day. I was supposed to get one hour each day. In the 360 hours of lockdown I was only allowed out of my cell a total of 4 hours in fifteen days and that's a violation in itself it was supposed to be 1 hour a day and just think I wasn't even a murderer. In the same fifteen-day period, during the first four days, I had no toilet tissue, no phone calls, no shower, and no exercise. I had four different cellmates. Only one left in intake for that long a period from the group that came in on May 17, 2010, after being processed on May 20, 2010.

I went to court on May 19, 2010, and the judge sentenced me to thirty days. The US Marshall put me back in the cell and told me to wait for paperwork from Judge Lee to be issued so they could take me back to jail. Three inmates with me have paperwork in hand,

and the marshal took us back to bullpen. I was the only one with no paperwork. While sitting in bullpen with about eighty-five other inmates, the correction officer started calling names of inmates that already have paperwork signed by prospective judges, telling them what the case outcome was, jail time, etc. After all inmates were gone, I and two other inmates were still sitting in bullpen, and I had no paperwork. After seeing the judge, the correction officer (at this time it was about 7:00 p.m.) kept coming around, asking my name, because she didn't have my paperwork. So at this time, I jokingly stated, "I guess since I don't have any paperwork, I am going to be released so I can go to work tonight."

    The female officer stated she was taking me back to the jail even though she didn't know what my status was. Violations needed to have the judge's signed order like the rest of the eighty-five inmates they took back prior. When they brought me back to the jail, I had no paperwork from the judge, and when I got processed on the next day, the C & P lady, Ms. Washington, didn't have the current paperwork from the judge on the previous day, so she processed me on the eight-year-old DWI charge, which was really an OWI. That would have meant a lower classification, which would have probably gotten me out sooner and to a less dangerous housing unit. She classified me to a medium housing unit instead of a minimum because of the no on the eight-year-old judge's order instead of the new order on May 19, 2010.

    This was an OWI thirty-day sentence during the fifteen-day stay in intake. I repeatedly ask for a nurse. They said "If you're not dying, you don't need one." Also, by being locked down almost the whole time, I felt unsafe, especially at night when they played loud radio music (96.3) over the PA system, so if I needed help, they couldn't hear me between the hours of 8:00 p.m. to 11:00 p.m. every night. I clearly thought this was an unsafe practice, and I was scared for my life, and it was so loud you couldn't hear yourself think, let alone call for help in case of emergency since the officer were in the bubble about two hundred feet away with no button or intercom within your cell to alert them of the dangerous or medical emergency violation. When I got to the housing unit on May 31, 2010, I had nine-year-old OWI charge. I was housed with drug dealers, carjacking, armed robbers, some murders, all types of people, although my only charge ever was a traffic violation. On the day of the trial, I pleaded with Judge Lee that I wasn't a convicted criminal and I didn't deserve to be in this inhumane condition at the jail and I had two minors at home alone. He still sentenced me to thirty days in jail after I told him it was a mistake, and I turned myself in because I never received the notice to appear in court.

I had a similar situation in Maryland, and my attorney or I didn't receive the notice, and they dismissed the charges after I turned myself in as in this trial. I told Judge Lee I was a thirty-one-year-old Federal employee, and he treated me like a criminal, so for this, I would like to file a civil suit against the DOC, DC government, DC Jail. When they brought me back from the court house that day, I was one of only three people on the big DOC bus, and one was a second-degree murderer, one had release papers in his hand, and myself with no paperwork, so clearly they had no authority to take me back to the jail without the order if it took them all night to find the paperwork. But then stated they were trying to get off, and it was getting late and they didn't care if they had it or not. During my brief stay at the DC Jail, most of the staff were unprofessional, obnoxious, and they stereotyped all black men as if they were hardened criminals.

Truly, as in my case, this was not true, so my objective was to let the public know that all black people were not criminals or convicts. I had been working for the federal government for thirty-one years, as I told the judge, and my case was nine years old. What do good tax-paying citizens who are law-abiding receive? And even in jail, I asked how I could reduce my sentence and get some good time. They told me I had to be here longer. You would think someone who had a job for thirty-one years and never been in trouble would get some credit, because it seems to me that the hard-core habitual offenders were given more chances for good time than the hard-working, law-abiding, tax-paying citizen like myself. Even murderers got good-time credit, and surely I was not that, and truly, this was an injustice. Also, while in intake unit, I had the same filthy sheets for sixteen days straight and the same underwear without being washed. I was in room temperature sometimes over one hundred degrees on some days. The first couple of days, I had to wipe my ass with the washcloth they gave me or continue to be constipated, so after three days, I used the bathroom and threw the rag away down the toilet bowl. The first time my sheets and towels were washed was on June 2, 2010, when I was in the NW3 housing unit after they moved me from lockdown, and I still had the same filthy underwear on they gave us when we got there on May 17, 2010. By June 2, 2010, they still hadn't washed the underwear, so I had to wash my underclothes by hand in the shower with regular body soap. Imagine that inhuman condition. The showers were either scalding hot or freezing cold. Try to take a shower in those conditions, let alone wash your clothes.

With most meals in intake unit, you got nothing to drink, and water coming from the sink in the cell was most of the time hot water. These conditions are not fit for dogs, let alone citizens with minor offenses. I believe it was because we were black males in a black city run by black administrations. They were treating us black men inhumanely because they could. This needs to stop now because even though most of the black men probably are guilty, they still are human and should be treated so. So I want to file a civil suit. I hope it will make them think twice before they act inhumanely if they get hit in the pocket with million-dollar lawsuit. They should have never put me in here. I asked the judge, but he wanted to treat me harshly for a nine-year-old minor traffic offense, which I thought could have been satisfied with a fine instead of jail time. When I finally got my sheets washed, they were literally black and stinking, smelling like vomit. Also, when I got to R & D and needed shoes to replace the ones they took from me, I told them I wore size 13. They said they didn't have any, so they gave me size 9. After that, the detail gentleman told me to go back and ask for my shoes from the officer, and he told me no, so I'd been wearing a size 9 for thirty days just because they were acting inhumanely, and that was how they treat black people. When we were in processing just before medical, they put the twenty-five of us in a cell on top of each other. Most of us were lying on a cold floor, asking for blankets. Because in R & D they made us shower, of course, our pores were open and it was cold, and they denied us that.

Only black officials were treating black people inhumanely because they thought they could get away with it. Case number 1: I rode to court on May 19, 2010. Everyone was shackled and handcuffed on DOC white bus. An inmate on narcotics said he had to go to the bathroom. He was young with long black beard. He came on the bus and said, "What's wrong?" So we spoke up for the old man and said he needed to use the bathroom. He came on the bus and yanked the old man off, and when he got to the gate, he slammed the old man's head against the steel gate, then took him in the back and came back and said, "Does anybody else want anything in a smart obnoxious manner?" as if to say, "I'll do the same thing to you if you act up." The federal marshals in DC Superior Court were mistreating people unnecessarily and without being provoked while they were shackled and handcuffed.

I worked at FBI Headquarters for six years, and you could have never told me the federal marshals were mistreating prisoners for no reason because they could get away with it. I was shackled when the inmates on the way over to the court were mumbling, "The marshals don't play. They'll beat you down for no reason at all," until I saw it for myself. They violate because it was black people they were mistreating, and it seemed like they got a laugh out of it and enjoyed it because they seemed to get away with it until I saw it. By being a former justice department employee, I knew if the DOJ knew of this, they would stop it immediately. I am going to make sure of it. Time is time, but being brutalized or inhumanely mistreated is something else. The way I see it, if they treated me inhumanely for a nine-year-old misdemeanor and I've never been in trouble, the rest of the black men are in a world of trouble. It needs to be brought to the surface so society could see, because anyone can make a mistake and get locked up, but it should not be a terrifying, brutal event, especially if they are law-abiding citizens like myself in for a traffic citation and never been in trouble all my life, and I am now fifty years old. Anyone can make a mistake. Besides, we all drive cars. Now back to the intake unit, I believe all the people here in the DC Department of Corrections did what they wanted no matter what the judge said. In my case, it was Judge Lee. Most of the staff, especially in places like the intake unit, ignores you because you are in your cell 23 sometimes twenty-four hours a day, and if they walk by and you ask for something, they talk smart, as this one older black lady I asked for help. She told me, "Shut up, you are just an inmate." I told this lady, "Ma'am, I have been working for the government for thirty-one years, and when I leave here, I am going to sue you, DC government, DOC, and DC Jail for the inhuman treatment and unprofessional gestures of the people in this jail atmosphere." I told her, "Everyone isn't a criminal, and I have been working for the government for as long as you have."

Only black people are treating black people inhumanly for no reason at all because they could, and it's got to stop now. Now as for gay people and jail sex, why on earth would you have homosexual men on the same block as the regular men? You have them on detail, which means they are roaming free within the unit, unsupervised to do whatever. On the day of the trial, the substitute lawyer, Mr. Cooper, who was court appointed and knew nothing about the case, was more or less telling me to go along with Judge Lee's decision. First of all, I told the judge that I left two minor children at home alone, with no phone and no supervision at all and no one to care for their well-being. The court-appointed lawyer told Judge Lee that, and he stated that the case was eight years old and a minor OWI and asked if I could pay the fine of $400 or serve my time on weekends. The judge wasn't hearing none of that, and after I told him I have never been in trouble never had a traffic ticket since then and been working for thirty-one years in the federal government with no regard for the minor children or my criminal record, he sentenced me to thirty days, which I thought was harsh, since I had no criminal record and no bad driving history.

Incarceration in DC Jail (May 17, 2010 to June 14, 2010)

Well, youngsters, this is a story that I hope will deter you from ever getting into trouble and having to come to a place such as this. First of all, I got here by trying to help my girlfriend get a police clearance in the District of Columbia so she could get her foster care license, not knowing that I had a nine-year-old traffic warrant still open. I paid money and submitted the information, and we went back upstairs to get the clearance. After about fifteen minutes, the man called my name but opened the door and said come on in. I knew right then and there something was up. This man said, "You have an open warrant for OWI, operating while impaired." I said, "Are you sure?" He said he checked twice and then said, "You are under arrest." I immediately called my girlfriend and told her they were arresting me. She said I thought you resolved that matter. I said I thought so too, so she said, "Do you want me to come get your stuff?" I said yes, and the saga began. The officer took all my personal belongings—jewelry, money, phone, shoelaces—and put the handcuffs behind my back and took me to CCB (Central Cell Block) MPD. They took me downstairs, and I saw these steel bars and beds with no mattress and roaches that were bigger than the inmates. It was hot and stuffy and dark. They took me before the judge, and the judge said no bond, so off to DC Jail I went. They called themselves, giving you some food—brown-bag baloney sandwiches that were old and stale. Then you never know who they will put in the cell with you. You don't want to be in a situation that you can't control, and that is just what's jail is about—no control of your life, from eating to sleeping to who they're going to put in your cell after the next one's gone, especially if you are in lockdown 24/7.

While on intake unit, I will take you on a cellmate-by-cellmate account of what goes on and how you might be subject to anything. Cellmate 1-J we call him. He was a real old-looking gentleman. It looked like the streets beat him down. Most times, when you enter a new cell, you almost always get the top bed, so that's what I got. Come to find out cellie number 1 was an alcoholic with the shakes.

He needed medicine to control his condition, so since we hardly got out, he was always hollering the nurse, but of course, this was DC Jail, so they hardly ever came, maybe once or twice. His charge was disobeying a stay-away order and bashing his wife's truck window in. He had four warrants for other stuff. Now remember, we were locked in 24/7, so now this old drunk had to use the bathroom. Oh brother, talking about shit stinking so bad that it made me vomit. I'm trying to tell him to flush the toilet. Now if you've ever been in a cell with the toilet, it's extremely hard to flush, so by his ass being a drunk and weak, he could hardly push the button, so now I was really suffering. So of course, mostly everyone has a court date or probation except for me. He went to court and came back with a partial cigarette. Remind you, smoking was prohibited, and it was contraband, so if we got caught smoking, I could possibly get another charge. This fool was hollering out the cell for a light, so I was saying to myself, "Please, I hope no one gives this man a light." He was really desperate for a cigarette, and if he got a light and he got caught, they might try to blame me, so now it was on. Thankfully, they moved him out about an hour later, and for the record, his old-looking ass was only forty-four, six years younger than me, oh brother.

Cellmate number 2, let's call him RK. He was a young man, about eighteen years old, dark skinned with dreads. His charge was larceny from a big stolen laptop computer. He thought no one saw him, but remember, youngster, first off, don't steal. Second, big brother's always watching. But the charge that got him in jail was unlawful entry. He said he and his cousin were camping out in a murder victim sister's house while she was in the witness protection program. On this night, she just happened to come back with a detective to get some clothes. Bam, they were inside. He got locked up. They called in his name, and a warrant came back out of Virginia. So he came to my cell on a 72 hour hold out of Va. Waiting to see if they were going to come and pick him up. He started telling me how he'd been in juvenile facilities all his life. He never knew his mother. She died at age three. His father had been locked up for fifteen years most of his adult life, so he had to steal to get what he wanted. I told him he didn't have to steal, just believe in God and do the right thing.

He kept saying, "Why does God keep doing bad things to me?" I told him, "Hold on one minute God doesn't treat people mean, and the devil is the other side of things." He started to understand. He said he had a lot of girls, and he was having sex unprotected. I told him, "These are not the old days and times. Protect yourself all the time. Bare sex kills." He kept saying he was dying, so I asked what was wrong. He said his side was hurting, and his balls were swollen. When you first get here, you get all the STD tests. The nurse called him to the infirmary and told him he had three STDs (chlamydia, gonorrhea, syphilis), and she told him, "Those girls out there are trying to kill you." He needed treatment, and he said he was scared of needles. I told him, "You should be glad that's all you have. They could give you a needle because it could be AIDS, and you will surely die." So I urge you, young people, use protection all the time. Save your own life. He also said he was bipolar and on meds.

Cellie number 3, we'll call him T, another one with a stay-away order. In his case, he went back over the woman's house the same day as the order was in effect. Stupid, but of course, it was due to alcohol. I call it ignorant oil because it makes you act ignorant.

Cellie number 4, we'll call him RS. He was in because of child support, but his case was unique. He was over fifty, educated but still in arrears for child support due to alcohol and drugs. He was so educated, but he was stupid. One thing I realized was that if you have children, you must pay for them in full, so that means they come first before anything. That's why I paid for my children voluntary with no hesitation and no interruptions so they can look up to me like I looked up to my father. So my advice to young adults there is that there is no reason for being incarcerated for something you have to do and you created. God will bless you all day long. Besides, if you get in arrears, you may never catch up. It was a day-to-day ritual that at three o'clock in the morning, they serve breakfast.

Well, I have only two days left, and I'm going to tell you the real story. First, the worst thing about prison/jail was everything, especially the unknown. What I mean is you never know what's next. For example, if your time is long, you don't know where or when they are going to move you. They can come at any time, day or night, and if you lose a cellie, you don't know who you are going to get next. By that, I mean a convict or inmate. And probably you say to yourself, "What's the difference?" Well, let me explain. A convict, for example, knows how to bid (do time), and with an inmate, you don't know how to do and you don't know what to expect, so if I had to get either, get me a convict. They have morals, and they respect you because we all have to be here (except me).

Let's go to food. Well, breakfast is at 3:00 a.m., lunch is at 10:00 a.m., and dinner is at 4:00 p.m., so that's how that is, and the food is horrible. For example, breakfast was cornflakes, one piece of bologna, and apple juice. Lunch could be anything, and sometimes, you don't get any meat. Dinner might be a little better, but at this point, I'm starving to death. I can't wait to get a steak and cheese sub. I tell you, young people, don't do crime unless you want someone to control all aspects of your everyday life, plus it's a waste of time, nonproductive in all ways. I'm writing this to tell you my experience so you don't have to do it. Also, in your cell, you don't know who's going to try to stab you with what they now call daggers, which used to be shanks, knives, etc. As I got to this point, I stayed in my cell most of the time. I only went out to shower in the morning and get my food trays, because for lunch and dinner you had to stand in line and hope you don't get in a fight.

The cell I was in now was my second and last and had dry shit on the walls, so that tells you the mindset of the people that had been in there. They actually wrote words and pictures in shit on the walls. I couldn't get out fast enough. Another aspect of jail life that I will never forget was the opening of the electric doors by the guard in the booth. If you wanted to get out, you had to wave your arms out the window of the doors and yell your cell number. By the way, none of the doors had glass in them by design, and that wasn't the bad part. The worst part was when the guard came by and had to physically close the doors by hand, which means slamming the doors. These doors were about an inch thick and made of solid steel, so imagine correction officers slamming eighty doors shut by hand. I'll probably still have nightmares of how loud the doors sound when being shut, and if you are asleep, it was even worst. I'll probably forever jump in my sleep, thinking I'm hearing doors shutting. Another thing was the hygiene items. The toothbrush was about and an inch long. I had to use it for a hairbrush also (a new unused one, of course). Hey, it was survival. I was leaving the game. Also, there were no mirrors, so I didn't see myself for thirty days. And for razors, well, when I got to the second block, I razor the first couple of days, and they collected them before second count. The second unit was a general population block, which means you come out most of the day but you go back in at court time, which was 8:00 a.m., 3:00 p.m., and 8:00 p.m. After you hear the court has been cleared, you were allowed to come back out. Most of time, court cleared in about one hour, and sometime it didn't, so you were stuck in.

Teens and adults, beware because you don't want to go there. Another aspect was the toilet bowl, which was solid steel, with the faucet designed to be used as a water fountain. Also, to me it felt like I've been drinking toilet water for thirty days since it was one unit. I didn't like that idea, but once again, don't go to jail. Better yet, don't do anything wrong so you won't have to go there. Also, there were no mirrors, so I didn't know how I look. I hoped I looked all right. All I did was read the Bible, work out, and write my story, in which I hope you will learn from it. My purpose for writing this part is to bring you to reality without having to be there. I've done it for you, and my crime was a nine-year-old traffic offense—OWI (operating while impaired). The judge just gave me thirty days with no strings attached. He could have given me probation, supervised probation, etc., but when I leave here, I'm free as it should be, because I have never been in trouble with the law. Also, showers have changed. They are individual, not open, so they are safer. No harm there, but you still have to watch your back. Remember, this isn't church, and these are not choir boys.

In general population, you have access to TV, basketball, playing cards, dominoes, and checkers. I never participated in any of them. The only sad part was my girlfriend never came to see me, but I know it was a good reason, and God kept us both, so this is the day God has made, so be glad to be in it. She is a good woman, and I love her. As in the Bible, this too shall pass. This has made me stronger, wiser, determined, and more patient than ever, so I see God can bring you through anything. I endured maximum lockdown, and I never thought I could do it, but God got me through with minding my business and being observant to the things around me. Also, by being prepared instead of scared. The toilet bowl was steel. Like I told you before, it was hard to sit on because it was ice-cold even with tissue on it. One other disturbing event was people hollering and screaming all night, especially when the count was unclear. They started cussing and screaming. If you didn't open the doors in a timely manner, they went berserk. Sometimes that was a bit disturbing, knowing if you didn't come to jail, you wouldn't need anyone to open doors for you. Let's describe the structure of the housing units as they call them (they are really cell blocks). Most cell blocks have 80 cells, 160 inmates, 2 tiers, 8 phones, and 8 showers, so you could imagine how things were. And don't bring the big juice container in the unit. Inmates would fight over the juice and almost riot, so, young people, if you don't want to go there and subject yourself to those conditions, don't commit crimes, or better yet, don't do anything wrong to put yourself in this environment.

My stepfather who used to be a correction officer always said, "If you go to jail for an hour, anything can happen, and you can spend the rest of your life, so don't go there." I was in a medium cell block, but most of the inmates were going to the feds (federal penitentiary) with long sentences, and DC does not have a federal penitentiary. So instead of inmates saying they can't wait to go home like me, they were saying, "I can't wait to go to the feds." It was a mess at this jail. Anytime an inmate says he can't wait to go to another prison instead of home, it's really bad there, horrendous. Another thing is, don't take or accept anything from anybody unless you can repay it or trade for it. You will get killed for one cookie around there. Trust and believe what I am saying; I've seen it for myself. I mind my business and stayed to myself. I never worried or was scared because I was prepared for anything at any time, so I just went about my merry way and did my time. Another thing is that these were actually criminals, repeat offenders, with most of them only an eighth-grade education. If that is so, my theory was you only get repeat criminals because they don't have any tools to get anything better for themselves or family. It was so sad. So, young people, get an education for yourself so you don't have to do crime.

One of the bright spots that I recognized was the medical services unit. First of all, it was free to all DC residents, and it was called Unity Health Services with eleven regular service offices in the DC area and three specialized offices, including one HIV facility, which I thought was great, and of course, it was the same medical unit that provided services to the jail. I blame the parents, school system, DC government for the education level of the 98 percent of the inmates at the jail. Now in addition, most of if not all of the inmates' population was black, so that should tell you a lot that somebody's not getting the perspective of recidivism. It's like a vicious circle that's never ending, and there's a monetary thing involved somewhere, but I haven't put that together yet. It seems like more inmates means more money for the state. I didn't like worrying about someone coming in to stab or attack me while sitting on the toilet bowl. That was a low in my stay, but I kept diligent and prepared. I also wondered about the inmate who turned religious all of the sudden after he gets in prison. I thought some of them were hypocrites. Before I came, I always prayed and sometimes read the Bible, so for me, it was normal, but for some, I wondered. I thought they needed to train these black men in some skills instead of sitting around all day, playing cards or watching TV. If they get training on the inside and make the best of their life while they are there, maybe they'll have a chance outside. It makes sense to me, because as long as they keep going back outside with nothing, they are going to come right back.

On the playing cards, I had noticed faces, so I asked who they were. They told me that the playing cards had the names and faces and descriptions of unsolved homicide victims dating back forty years now. That was amazing because no one was going to tell after all were in jail.

Traffic Court

Do the right thing always. Respect. Let's start from the beginning. I had court date for traffic violation. The previous court appearance was the first one. The judge in the court house in Upper Marlboro, Maryland, for traffic cases will tell you specifically on the first date that unless you want to represent yourself, they will continue the case, but the next time you come to court for this case, you better retain a lawyer. So I left the courthouse, and I retained a lawyer. Mr. Powell, I paid the man $1,500. It was $750 to represent me in court and $750 to keep my license at MVA in the state of Maryland. When you get a traffic violation, there are two separate issues. So when all is said and done, you have to go to two hearings. One is the court, and the other at the MVA.

Getting ready for court date, I did what I was supposed to do. Now on the day of court, my lawyer wasn't in the courtroom when I got there or he had not gotten there at the start of the proceedings and when he got to my name. All these young men walked up there to the bench to plead their case, and not one of them had a lawyer. When he got to my name, I walked up there behind all these guys with no lawyer, and the judge automatically expected me not to have one. That's why he was shaking his head, so as I approached, I asked him, "Your Honor, why are you shaking your head?" He stated, "I see you don't have representation [counsel] either." I told that judge, "Hold on, Your Honor. The last time I was here, they told me to retain an attorney, and I did." The judge said, "Well, where is he?" I told the judge, "I don't know," but I also told the judge, "You only told me to retain the attorney, not to go by his house to pick him up." The court room laughed, and so did the judge. The judge asked me what the lawyer's name was. I told him, and he told me to go sit in the back and he would try to find him. So as court proceedings got well underway, I looked up and through the door, and my attorney came in. The judge stopped proceedings for a minute and said, "Mr. Jones, you found your attorney." I stated, "No, Your Honor, I haven't moved except for almost going to jail for not having one at the time you called me. I saw you're here I never moved the lawyer found me and it is about time. They dismissed the case. Thank God.

Helping Hands and Shoot-Out

Once again, I'm writing about how young adults, teenagers, or children should expect to happen when you live malice-free. Treat others like you want to be treated so as not to bring harm to yourself or family. Like karma, what comes around goes around. Treat everyone right. God will protect you, but if you don't beware, don't wonder why many things are going wrong in your life.

In July 2013, on a Sunday night, I was looking out the window and saw a gentleman who looked like he had car problems. He had his hood up, so since I work on cars as a hobby, I thought I would go out and give the gentleman a hand. When I got to the top of the steps, I asked what was wrong. He stated that it was his daughter's car, and it wouldn't shut off. By the way, it was a brand-new car, so the first thing I told him was, "We need to disconnect the battery." I pleasantly asked what happened, and he stated that the car had been in a shooting. It didn't faze me at the time because I was trying to help him shut the car off. We unhooked the battery cables; it still wouldn't shut off. We accidentally hit the battery with a socket wrench, and that shut the car down.

My Lexus was parked I guess five cars down from his, so once we shut the car off, we said our pleasantries, and he thanked me. He noticed I had a New York accent. I told him I came from New York City. I went back to my car to put the tools I used to help him away. When I got to my trunk and put the tools away, I sat in my car and put the shade back. I looked out the passenger window and saw this gentleman shooting from a TEC-9. I couldn't see in front because the shade was in the window, so I got out of my car and looked over the roof to see who he was firing at. Unbeknownst to me, there were some guys shooting directly in my direction. They were rolling around the parking lot toward our direction, shooting the whole time. I didn't know that the guy shooting back actually saved my life because I had no idea (no gun) what was going on, but if that guy next to my passenger door did shoot back, these guys coming around the parking lot would have shot me dead, and all I was trying to do was help. So I tell all young people that it's okay to help people, but pay attention around you because, like I always tell young adults, anything can happen at any time. Be prepared and not scared; it may save your life. During this shoot-out, approximately forty bullets passed around, over, under me with five different. That means five different people had different guns out there, and not one bullet hit me, my car, or anything, so I thank God like always. And yes, I believe in him and the best of my ability to do the right thing. I treat people right or how I want to be treated. So when stuff like this happens, don't mess your own chances up by living cruddy or taking advantage of people or deliberately mistreating people so your life will be long and prosperous.

Getting Cigarettes for Girlfriend

On this Saturday night, I went out to my girlfriend's house to visit and clean my Lexus. It was a summer's night, warm and a little breezy. It was a nice night for cleaning my car. When I finished, she said she was going to follow me back to my house. So I followed. From the time I left her house, she was having a nicotine fit, in which she needed a cigarette. She kept bugging me about a cigarette. I told her to stop at a nearby gas station on her side of town. I never stopped at any other gas station unless it was where I live at. I don't smoke, so there was no need to stop anywhere else to get gas. So we stopped at this gas station to buy her some cigarettes. I tell you, I don't pay for their habit, but this time, she needed a little help, so I told her, "I'll get them." We pulled into the gas station. She was in front of me. I got out and went to her car to talk to her about the cigarettes. We start arguing, so I said "Forget it, I'll get them." I proceeded to the outside window and purchased the cigarettes. When I turned around, there was a pistol in in face, and I went to back up and a shot gun was sticking in my back. I threw the cigarettes and change up in the air and shouted, "I don't have any money." All the while, I dashed to her car, which was in front of mine. I told her to pull off because someone had to be around to tell what had happened. Thank God. PS: my biggest thing is how my girlfriend would explain to my mother that I got shot for buying cigarettes and I didn't smoke. Oh brother.

Child Support: Baby Momma Drama (Do the Right Thing)

In February 2009, I was sitting in the barber shop, and my phone rang. I couldn't answer the phone right then due to the razor on my head, so I waited until I got out of the chair to call voicemail to see who called. I didn't recognize the number. When I called back, the person on the voicemail said, "Sheriff's Department, Child Enforcement Division." I called back, realizing that my son would be eighteen in ten months, getting ready to graduate in June of that year. Ten months but didn't turn eighteen until that next January 3, so I said my son was almost grown, and I shouldn't/couldn't be there for him. I took care of my son and her other kids without the courts; I called to see any children I didn't know about. When I called the sheriff back, I asked what the child's name, and he said my son's name. I told the sheriff he was almost grown. So now I was mad as hell because I helped with the other kids when they were not mine. Imagine, I was a black man doing the right thing and look where I still end up. Be sure to pay in money orders or any form just keep receipts you just may need them ask me I wound up in court 17 years later imagine if I did not keep my money order receipts like my Dear mother told me you just never know CYA Cover Your A.

Words of Wisdom

Young adults raising children and their diets. When we were young, when we went shopping to the grocery store with our father, my sisters and I were allowed to get our own grocery carts, and he told us to get whatever we liked as long as we got meats and veggies and anything else we liked. So when we got home, we couldn't ever say there wasn't anything in the house we liked to eat because we had a chance to get whatever we wanted to eat. He always used to say food bills cost less than doctor bills, and these days, there is no comparison, which means if you eat a well-balanced diet, your children will be a lot less sickly and they won't be going to the hospital as much if at all, except for regular checkups. This is not to say kids can't eat fast food, but keep it to a minimum. As far as I can remember, growing up, we hardly ever got sick, except for chicken pox and measles. Prepare home-cooked healthy meals for your children so they will look forward to coming home to Mom's cooking.

Jealously-Envy-Ladies and Gentlemen throughout my life I've seen people exemplify sins of jealously or envy of either who someone is or what they have. Now about who someone is just be all you can for yourself then you will not have time worrying about who someone is. Now about what someone has first just acquire what your heart desires and once again doing this you won't have time worrying about what someone has. Second whatever material item it is that someone has I am positively one hundred percent sure the make more than one of that particular item no matter what it is. As I said throughout my book as with anything else in life how bad do you want it and what are you willing to sacrifice to achieve it. So what I am telling you is that you never have to be jealous or envious of anyone or anything that they have because you can do it and have the same. Don't never sell yourself short. STAND STRONG AND TALL.

Peer Pressure-Gossip-Character Assassination-First off everyone has a mouth (see pg 76 illus) and their own opinion so never worry about what people think and say about you as long as you know you're doing the right thing and living right never worry about what someone says or thinks about you because if you do that means you think more of what someone says or thinks about you than you think of yourself and that should never be. Always think highly of yourself while doing the right thing. Second always remember if someone is

THE BOTTOM LINE

talking about you and you know who you are and are living right DISMISS IT. Also remember from what I read and experienced it is said that out of the million subjects in the world to talk about they are talking about you BOY ARENT YOU VERY IMPORTANT. Keep FOCUSED on who you are and what you want to be in life. Do Good.

Teens and young adults or anyone whom this applies, this is my parting advice, which might save you or your family's life. Throughout my book, I tried to tell or advise you on how it's a must to live right and do the right thing, which is the right thing to do. But sometimes, trouble (either accidentally or being at the wrong at the wrong time) might come your way. So my advice to you is always remember that anything can happen anytime or anywhere. No matter where you are and no matter what you are doing, be prepared, not scared. I am not saying walk around paranoid. Just keep in the back of your mind that things can happen and sometimes will.

For example, my fiancée at the time and I took a trip to see my mother in New York on Staten Island for the first time. I was thirty, and she was nineteen. When we got off the Goethals Bridge at Forest Ave. We decided to go to the Forest Ave. Shopping Center. I was driving a 320 I BMW without of state tags, but this was home to me. When we got out of the car at the mall, I observed three men looking at us as we got out of our car. One was a short man and two six foot-eight guys. Getting in the mall, I noticed the three guys following us. At this time, my fiancée, being young, was trying to wander off. I noticed one of the guys following her and the other two following me, so now I rushed to get my fiancée. Now she was with me, and the guys were still following us. Now remember I was home, so I got closer to the short guy. Once he saw who I was and recognized I was a friend of the family, the robbery was off. I was sure if they didn't know us, they were going to rob us, so what I'm saying is anything can happen anytime, and that's the bottom line.

So pay attention to your surroundings. PS: the short guy was a known bank robber who went to jail for such.

Teens and young adults, the old saying that the lazy person works the hardest clearly means that when approaching any task when you try to take shortcuts or try to speed through the tasks, most of the time what I experienced when I was a young man was either the end result is less than what I wanted or I still wind up having to do it again. So I try to do it the right way the first time. What I'm saying is it really doesn't pay to be lazy in the long run. It's not a good habit to add to anyone's life's regiments. When I approach anything I want, what I have to do is be about it, which means get it done.

This goes to all mankind, whether you are a little child or adult and in between. This also holds true for the rich or poor and in between. This also holds true for the educated and uneducated and for all nationalities and colors. When coming to an agreement or disagreement, I want all mankind to always remember that in any situation, there's only one resolution—the right way and the wrong way, not my way or your way. If everyone takes this approach, the world would be one heck of a better place to live, and that's the real bottom line.

Teens and young adults, remember one thing. When you are born, you are on God's time, and it says that there's a time to be born and a time to die. This is in the Bible, and in between these two clauses comes all the other things we do in life. So God already has a successful plan for you. Don't mess it up with foolishness or by letting the devil put his plan in place.

Words of wisdom, last but not the least important, while growing up in New York City on Staten Island (the Rock), I used to hear older guys always saying "Word is bond." I didn't know what it meant. So one day I asked. They told me it meant that when someone says something, it means whatever they told you was the truth. So what I'm telling you is keep your word good. That means give people the correct information to best to your knowledge and not purposely misleading people, because when you first meet anyone, all you have is your word—make it count. When people talk to you, they can see through the BS anyway. Always tell the truth and shame the devil.

Respect

Always remember that money can buy a lot of things. The one thing it cannot buy is respect. Young people respect must be earned. People may like you because of your money. They may even befriend you but that does not mean they respect you.

Trust

First of all, if you really want one hundred percent positive results as far as trusting someone is concerned then learn to place your trust in the Lord. Since we live among humans, we must place our trust in those closest to us. We all must trust someone either in our personal and business lives. While growing up on the ROCK Staten Island in New Brighton, I was taught to never trust anyone. You never know what people are thinking, what their motive is; and what their heart is like. I keep friends to a minimum. Make sure everyone is on the same level.

I never really trust anyone especially with my woman and my money especially when you have the best of one and a lot of the other. For some reason people start acting strange and funny when it comes to a woman and money. So watch this personal and business aspect of your life because you can be sure others will.

Secrets

We all have them. If you never want your secrets told then tell no one. I learned that when I was a young man. While having an affair with a woman at work, when no one even suspected we knew each other, she told me "If you never want a secret known, never tell anyone." She stipulated "never tell anyone" then you never have to worry about it coming back to haunt you. So watch who you trust. Watch what secrets you tell and to whom you tell them. At the Bureau, it was based on need to know basis. On the streets, the saying was "I would tell you a secret but I might have to dispose of you." So you see the importance of watching your lips.

Long Term Planning vs. Short Term Planning

Young people, I plead with you because you are young and have your entire life ahead of you, "Do not short change yourself and your future by living day-to-day." I see some of you do just that. Please plan for the future. You will attain more. Rome and success were not built in a day.

Tough Guy/Girl Persona

Young people, there are only two places for these types of people – Death and Jail. You better make damn sure that whatever you do, be prepared to accept the consequences. Think real long before you do so wrong that it cant be repaired or rectified think long and hard because some things cant be reversed.

A So-Called Bad Situation

Young people, please remember that in any bad situation in life something good always comes out of it – if nothing more than a learned lesson. But if you pay attention to the what, when, where, why and how the situation occurred then you will see something good out of most bad situations. Look for it. It is there. Think outside the box.

Life's Adjustment

What this means is that in life there will most definitely be obstacles, good and bad luck, and ups and downs. Society tries to put a monkey wrench in your plans. Instead of panicking, worrying, or stressing out, just make a suitable adjustment to keep on track. ADJUST, ADJUST, AND ADJUST. It can be done only if you are doing the right thing.

Seeking Success, Riches and Wealth

First of all, you must see yourself in these capacities. I have always envisioned myself wealthy. You must do the basics in acquiring the knowledge of these types of people, i.e. attending free Get Rich seminars and reading get rich books written by authors such as Napoleon Hill. Reading these types of books will teach you to think outside the box about acquiring wealth. These are the only types of books I have read all my life. There is a big difference between work money and water money. Work money is when you work a job for a set salary. Water money is when you get money twenty-four hours a day, seven days a week and three hundred sixty-five days a year. For example, publishing a book in the 21st century. The possibilities and money are endless. Think about it. What would you rather do purchase something for a million dollars or earn the same. In the books I read, it said you will never be rich working a job. But the money you make from a job and where you invest it, now you have hit the jack pot. Good Luck.

Taxes

Young people when I was young, my father used to tell me, "Son, the only two things you are guaranteed in life are death and taxes." As long as you live life the right way and do the right thing, God will keep you. Pay your taxes on time and in full. Never cheat, please. I mean never. It will cost you in the future in earnings and interest. Most of all, it will reduce your purchasing power for you, your family and things you might need, i.e. a house, a car or anything else you might desire. These will be out of reach or limit. What you would normally be able to afford you cannot because you owe back taxes with interest. Get professional help if you are not sure how to prepare your taxes. God will not hold good things from you. Along with prayer, hard work and good decision-making, you can get what you need and want without cheating.

Money

Some young people might have heard someone saying the old adage, "Money won't make a person happy." In some cases this may be true not many in the books. I read, "Try to be happy without enough money especially for the basics in life for you and your family's existence." Do not be a fool young people. You need money and plenty of it. As I see it, nothing has ever gotten cheaper or cost less. Everything has always increased. To even live comfortable in the 21st century, you need (dough) money. Do not let anyone tell you otherwise. How do you want to live?

Housing

Young people, I know that in this day and time housing is expensive. When starting out, you might have to have roommates as I did until you start making some money. Make damn sure your name is on the lease to ensure that you have stable arrangements. In doing this, no one can evict you for whatever or whenever they want. Remember, this is just a stepping stone. The next move – your own place.

Personal Conduct: Rules for Success

Engaged in conversation when talking to someone you know or don't know. If the person you are talking to asks you something you feel is inappropriate or just none of their darn business, first of all, you don't have to answer at all, but if you think they have bad intentions or you are curious, do what they taught me as a young fella growing up on Staten Island (the Rock). Kindly ask them why they are asking you whatever it is they're asking. If you get any response other than the right one, you know that person doesn't mean you any good. Shut them down kindly; they are fishing.

When I was nineteen or twenty, we had a roommate who was attending Howard Law School. He was one of the wanted men on campus at that time, which means he was getting a lot of girls to the apartment. I asked what he was taking to keep up his strength. He said he used ginseng root extract. Anything associated with this natural male enhancer does a lot of good for the body, including general health, without side effects, thus contributing to overall good health. It works. I've been using ginseng extract for forty years.

Research the ginseng health benefits for yourself to be truly amazed. There's only one small negative thing about ginseng; it doesn't taste like Cool-Aid, but of course, most things that work don't taste good. Work wonders. After a while, you'll get used to the taste like I did, especially when you know it does the whole body good.

Words of Wisdom

When we were young, our grandmother was our caretaker while our parents worked. I knew I could ask my grandmother anything, so I asked her about my favorite pastimes, girls. My grandmother told me, "Grandson, watch who you get in the bed with, because you might have to look at and deal with this person one way or the other all your life due to having a child with that person. Protect yourself first from STD and second from having child that you are probably not ready or be able to take care of anyway. Besides it's better to be married anyway. Remember, marriage is honorable by God, and that is in the Bible."

Men we all love those fine sexy women we like their hair smile physical shape and all those things that make us attracted to women, but remember (Those Drawers are the cause of it all. Don't let those DRAWERS get you in trouble by doing something you might later regret it's not worth it there are more than one pair of drawers in the world stay free to see. But always remember, those drawers get us in trouble. It's not worth it. You'll regret it later.

Women do not fear I did not forget about you all my dears and I did not want you to think I left you out. Previously I warned the

Men about those women Drawers, now I have something to warn women about. Women don't let a man's piece of wood make you do something that is not too good and make you also do something that you might regret or can't reverse later and that might land you too in a place that's really not good. THINK.

Managing Money (Spending Money While Saving Money)

I was in the grocery store one morning, standing at the checkout counter, and struck up a conversation with an elderly woman. She told me that one way to save money when purchasing any item is to set a spending limit while still buying what I want. Spend no more that I said I was going to spend and not a penny more, and I won't feel bad about what I purchased while saving money all the time.

Money and Charity-Giving

As far as charitable contributions, my grandmother used to tell me when I was young, "If your fists are closed, no money goes out, and at the same time, no money can get in. Don't miss your blessings. Give what you can but give. Remember, I didn't say go broke."

As for life's retrospect regarding my grandmother, the last time I spoke with my grandmother before she passed (God bless her soul), I was doing as she said by saying my prayers every day. She told me that day, "That is a good thing, grandson, but these days, you have to pray all day long." And just think I thought I was doing something.

Your thought process when looking at a price on something. Always remember that everything has a cost, so whatever the price is, all you have to do is earn enough to afford it. Don't fret. Find a way. I got that advice from my lawyer friend at eighteen years old.

Managing Money (Credit)

Teens and young adults, good credit is very important to have because in this day and time, you can't always purchase big ticket items with cash. Don't overspend or overextend your credit, and always pay your bills before time so as to keep your credit rating good. Borrowing money will cost you less as far as interest rate is concerned.

THE BOTTOM LINE

This is an Annual family picnic at my aunt Dots job at the infamous Willow Brook State Mental Institution as you might be able to see there are a lot of the mentally challenged on the grounds and they were unpredictable as a young boy I felt unsafe and was always on guard out there so as I got older I told my parents I was not going out there anymore and they did not make me go anymore thank God.

> IF YOU'RE NOT PART OF THE SOLUTION
>
> YOU'RE PART OF THE PROBLEM

> SMALL MINDS TALK ABOUT OTHER PEOPLE
>
> MEDIOCRE MINDS TALK ABOUT ADVS, NEWSPAPER, TV
>
> BRILLANT MINDS TALK ABOUT IDEAS

THE BOTTOM LINE

YOU ARE NOT BETTER THAN ANYONE AND NO ONE IS BETTER THAN YOU

Why Worry?

There are only two things to worry about; either you are well or you are sick.

If you are well, then there is nothing to worry about;

But if you are sick, there are two things to worry about; either you get well or you will die.

If you get well, there is nothing to worry about.

If you die, there are only two things to worry about; either you will go to Heaven or Hell.

If you go to Heaven, there is nothing to worry about;

But if you go to Hell, you'll be so damn busy shaking hands with friends,

You won't have time to worry!

CHILDREN
Tired of being Harrassed by your Stupid Parents? **ACT NOW!** Move out, Get-A-Job Pay Your Own Bills, While You Still Know Everything.

Domestic Violence

I almost forgot, young adults, old fools (that's right, I said old fools), when I was young, my mother and father used to physically fight when drinking on weekends. It scared me and my sisters to death. I hated it, but I was too young to do anything. First off, it makes children scared, frightened, and just plain terrified, so I beg you, do not to fight or argue or any of that foolishness that alters children's innocent mental state of mind. Children are not born terrified and scared. That's a learned behavior. There's nothing worse than children witnessing two people that they love physically harming each other. Don't let your children think that this is a normal way of life. *It is not.* Due to my witnessing my parents fight, I never did that to my kids, and they grew up fine as it should be. Figure out another more peaceful resolution.

THE BOTTOM LINE

This a picture of George C Cromwell basketball gym located minutes from my neighborhood on Staten Island NY this at this time was one of the biggest gyms in NY with 12 full courts located minutes from the SI ferry and with that came some of the best ball players from all 5 boroughs the competition was a beast.

This is me on graduation day in June 1980 standing by my first car a 1972 Blue Ford Pinto 4 spd which my parents got for me and they made me pay them back and relinquished all of the responsibilities for the car to me which I was glad to take and drove that car to school everyday and everywhere else and if nothing else it made me keep a part-time job of some sorts because my parents had nothing else to do with my car, gas indeed, insurance nothing. So that really helped me to responsible at a young age.

Me and my siblings

Me and my son Jaron Jones
on his High School Graduation Day

About the Author

Bruce Andrew Jones was born on August 8, 1961, in Harlem Hospital in Manhattan, New York, to his parents, Moses Andrew (Jack) Jones and Lillian C. Jones. He grew up in Staten Island, New York, in the Jersey Street Projects, next to Mahoney Playground, with his two successful baby sisters, Lisa and Denise. He attended Curtis High School in Staten Island and moved to Dumfries, Virginia, where he graduated from Garfield Senior High School in 1980. Bruce played basketball at both high schools. He began his federal career at the FBI Headquarters in Washington, DC, January 1981. He transferred to the United States Postal Service (USPS). During this time, he graduated from Control Data Institute, where he studied computers, electronics, and technology. He is known in the Washington, DC, metropolitan area as New York for his New York accent, playing basketball, spinning tables in the DC Metropolitan area, and of course, pushing those high-end luxury automobiles—Benz and BMW. He presently drives a Lexus LS. Nothing like it.

www.ingramcontent.com/pod-product-compliance
Lightning Source LLC
Chambersburg PA
CBHW060409080526
44583CB00012B/514